Nuffield–BP Business for Intermediate Part One GNVQ

Published by HarperCollins Publishers Limited
77–85 Fulham Palace Road
Hammersmith
London W6 8JB

www.**Collins**Education.com
On-line Support for Schools and Colleges

First published 2000

British Library Cataloguing in Publication Data
A catalogue record for this publication is available from the British Library.

ISBN: 000 329099 9

Commissioned by Charis Evans
Edited by Brigitte Lee
Design and typesetting by Visual Image
Project management and cover design by Patricia Briggs
Printed and bound by Scotprint

You might also like to visit:

www.**fire**and**water**.com
The book lover's website

Contents

Unit 1 – How businesses work

* material differs from foundation level

* material differs from foundation level

The **in tray** asks questions that focus students' thinking on the ideas developed in the case study.

The **text** provides a general explanation of the particular business issues of the spread, and provides the necessary preparation for assessment.

Checkpoints are straightforward questions designed to check student comprehension.

Key points round off most spreads, providing a checklist of the terms students need to know.

Portfolio prompts remind students that they can relate what they have just learnt to their ongoing investigations of real businesses. They encourage them to build into their portfolio work relevant aspects of these businesses.

In the future

Better motorway systems and improved communications through mobile phones, Ceefax and the like mean that many businesses worry less about location.

The use of the telephone has changed the way that many businesses operate. **On-line shopping** also makes use of the telephone, linked to a computer with a modem. Organisations do not need to have shops where customers can view the items on sale. Customers from all over the country, or even the world, can have access to the same products or services.

An on-line business order has to be translated into actual products. A warehouse and transport service will be necessary at some stage. Electronic orders rely on the customer using a bank account or credit card. This means that the system has to be able to prevent fraud. It also means that businesses will not have any young customers. (You have to be an adult with a good bank account to use a credit card.)

Shopping on the Internet is a growing area and is likely to have a big influence on the way we shop in the future.

IN TRAY

1 Why do you think Direct Line's method of selling insurance over the telephone has been so successful?

2 Why does Direct Line not need to locate its centres close to where all of its customers live?

3 Why do you think the telephone might not have been so successful ten years earlier?

In addition, Hawkshead uses other ways of gaining more customers: it offers a **mail-order shopping** service, telephone orders and on-line shopping through the Internet. Customers pay using their credit or debit card.

TRAY

ny different ways can a goods from Hawkshead? o say that Hawkshead cate anywhere?

3 Which sales method do you think will be most widely used in ten years time?

CHECKPOINT

1 What are the advantages for businesses of selling on the Internet or by telephone?

2 What are the advantages for customers of shopping on the Internet?

3 What is likely to be the problem for someone under 18 trying to buy some clothes on the Internet?

KEY TERMS

• **Mail-order shopping** is using a catalogue to buy and sell goods through the post.

• **On-line shopping** is buying goods or services through the Internet.

PORTFOLIO PROMPTS

Find out if the business you are investigating has a website. If so, what is it for?

117

Using this book in the classroom

The book provides coverage of all aspects of what students need to learn for Part One Business, together with a range of ways in which they can reinforce their understanding. Key skills are all covered in the Teacher's Resource Pack, which contains activities supporting the teaching of key skills, as well as the development of portfolio evidence.

As the foundation and intermediate specifications are 'nested', there is a close match between this book and the foundation book. Matching spreads in the two books always start with the same case study and have as much common content as possible.

Where the specifications diverge, two strategies have been adopted. When there is more material on the same topic for intermediate than there is for foundation, extension spreads in this book have been designated a, b, c, etc. Where different material is covered at each level, spreads are marked with an asterisk. Wherever possible, any additional material has been positioned at the end of a unit. When this occurs, the numbering simply continues.

Acknowledgements

The publishers would like to thank the following for permission to reproduce photographs and artwork in this book:

ACAS, p. 29; Ace Photo Agency, pp. 92 (x3), 109 (x4); Airtours, p. 140; Alton Towers, p. 170 (x3); Anglia Railways, p. 88 (x4); Anglia Sporting Activities, p. 94 (x3); Appletree Cottage, pp. 134, 138; ASDA, p. 30; Ron Bagley, p. 96 (x3), 103; Bakers Dolphin, p. 13; James Beattie plc., pp. 131, 139; Birds Eye Wall's, pp. 84, 86 (x2), 143; The Body Shop, p. 135; Boots plc, p. 11; Britax, pp. 180–1 (x3); British Aerospace, pp. 9, 13; Britvic, pp. 60–1 (x4); Bruce Coleman Collection, pp. 97, 109; Burger King, p. 135; Cadbury's, pp. 44, 156–7 (x3), 159 (x2); J. Allen Cash Ltd, pp. 93, 108 (x3); Steve Chester, pp. 48 (x2), 49; Chester Zoo, pp. 22, 23, 53, 58 (x2); Clarks, p. 135; Courts, p. 70 (x5); Department of Trade and Industry, p. 28; Direct Line, p. 116–117 (x3); Eastern Generation, pp. 14, 24; EasyJet, pp. 128 (x3), 129, 138; Farmers Weekly Picture Library, p. 35; Fort Shopping Park, pp. 118, 119; Fox's, pp. 78, 79; Future Publishing, pp. 13, 18 (x3); GettyOne Stone: pp. 2 (Peter Dean), 7 (Lonnie Duka), 79 (Bruce Ayres), 90 (Michael Rosenfeld), 109 (Michael Rosenfeld), 152 (Jeremy Walker), 160 (Andre Perlstein), 161 (Carol Ford), 192 (Moggy); Granada, p. 95 (x4); Grattan, p. 82; Gremlin Group plc, pp. 4–5 (x5), 6 (x4), 7, 11, 154 (x2); John Harris (NUJ), p. 35; Hartland Evening News, pp. 120–1 (x4); Hawkshead, p. 116; Health and Safety Executive, pp. 32, 33 (x5); Hulton Getty, p. 171; Kappa SSK Ltd, p. 104; Laura Ashley, p. 151; Lawson Mardon Starr, pp. 42 (x2), 44; LDV, p. 106 (x2); Magna Specialist Foods, p. 26 (x2); Manchester United Football Club, pp. 147, 179; Marks & Spencer plc, p. 11; Bethan Matthews: pp. 8, 9, 28, 76 (x2), 80 (x6), 100 (x2), 132, 144, 146 (x2), 168, 190, 191, 204, 205, 207, 212, 213; The National Trust Photographic Library, pp. 52 (x2), 63; Nestlé, p. 45; Next plc., pp. 211, 220; Orange plc, pp. 186–7 (x5); Oxfam, pp. 16, 17; Perrier, pp. 142, 220; Pizza Hut, p. 3; Post Office, pp. 84, 135, 136–7 (x6); Professional Footballers Association, p. 34; Redken, p. 48 (x3); Rover Group, pp. 2, 85, 90; J. Sainsbury plc, pp. 11, 188; Severn Valley Railway Company, p. 50 (x4); Skyscan Photo Library, p. 96; Sunderland AFC, pp. 36, 40, 41, 155 (x2); Tesco plc, pp. 13, 110, 149, 188, 189; Transport and General Workers Union, p. 34; Trevor Perry Environmental Images, p. 110; Jenny Tyler, pp. 46, 47 (x2); Unilever, pp. 182–3 (x3); Unipart, p. 2; Welsh Development Agency, pp. 114, 115; West Midlands Co-operative Society Ltd, pp. 132, 139; WHSmith, pp. 67, 72.

Every effort has been made to contact copyright holders, but if any have been inadvertently overlooked, the publishers will be pleased to make the necessary arrangements at the first opportunity.

Almost all the case studies in this book are real. Some businesses and people are given their real names and have genuine photographs as well. Others have been given different names to protect their identity. In these cases, the photographs are for educational purposes only and are not intended to identify the individual. The publishers cannot accept any responsibility for any consequences resulting from this use of photographs and case studies, except as expressly provided by law.

A product of partnership

Many people have helped to make this book possible. The editors were Paul Clarke, Jenny Wales and Nancy Wall. They also contributed to the writing process. They were supported by a large team of teacher writers: Marian Ellard, Tim Fisher, Glynis Frater, Steve Packer, Neil Reaich, Jenny Smart and Richard Young. The recent experience and imaginative ideas of this team were invaluable in making the book lively and varied in its approach. Duncan Cullimore helped by reading and commenting on the finished spreads.

The Collins Educational staff provided a great deal of help and support before, during and after the writing process. Patricia Briggs and Charis Evans were both a great source of strength and ideas.

Writing the book was made possible by the funding from the Nuffield Foundation and BP. Both organisations gave unstinting support while leaving the authors completely free to pursue educational objectives.

The help and support of our administrator, Linda Westgarth, whose contributions were so many and so great that they cannot be briefly described, were essential to both the development work and the final preparation of the book for publication. We would also like to thank our partners, who have helped in many ways.

1 What is a business?

OBJECTIVES

To learn that there are many different sorts of business.

To look at ways in which they are similar and different.

IN TRAY

Some of the businesses in these photographs have something in common.

1 Which of these businesses are near where you live?

2 Write down the numbers of those you think can be grouped together, and say why you think this.

3 Which photos belong to more than one group? Write down what they show and explain why they are in each group.

Businesses come in all shapes and sizes. Some have things in common, and others are connected in different ways. These photographs help us to see these links and connections. To use them we will need to sort them into groups. We might group them according to ownership, size, those which are in a similar line of business, or those with strong links between them. For example, the cattle farm, the burger manufacturer and the hamburger take-away are clearly linked. They form a **production chain**.

The photographs don't tell us everything, but they provide a window through which we can look to explore businesses. You'll find other examples of how this can be done later in the book. On each double page, look for the following features.

◆ **In tray** – helps you to understand the material.

◆ **Action box** – asks you to carry out various tasks.

◆ **Portfolio prompts** – provide suggestions to support your investigations.

◆ **Checkpoint** – asks you to show that you understand the material.

ACTION

Survey your local area to explore the types of businesses there. You may use a map and, if possible, a digital camera to record your results. Discuss the best way of doing this with your teacher.

KEY TERM

🔑 A **production chain** shows the links between getting raw materials for a product, turning those materials into the product, and, finally, selling the product.

PORTFOLIO PROMPTS

What sort of business are you going to investigate? Make a short list of ones that interest you.

3

2 Getting going

Gremlin
Group Plc

A small beginning

Ian Stewart worked for Dixons. The shop was often full of young people looking for computer games. Although many just came in to play, sales were good. Had there been more room on the shelves for the right sort of games, sales would have been even better.

An idea came to Ian. Why not open a shop that specialised in computer games? Ian rented a shop in Carver Street in Sheffield, and set up Just Micro. He stocked a wide range of games, so there was something to appeal to everyone. The rent was low and he did not need many staff. The takings were good and Ian was making a profit. The business was a success.

AHEAD OF THE GAME

JUST MICRO
COMPUTER SOFTWARE SPECIALISTS
COMPUTERS FOR FUN

IN TRAY

1   Why was it a good idea to set up a computer games shop?

2   How do you think Ian decided on the type of games to sell?

3   Look at the picture of the shop. Do you think the rent was high or low? Why?

4   What does Ian have to do in order to make a profit?

Ian Stewart saw an opportunity and took it. His **enterprising** nature helped. But before doing anything, he had to decide whether the shop would make money. Once he had decided that it would pay its way, there were many things to be done before he could open the shop.

ACTION

1   How do you think Ian decided that the shop would make money? What questions would he have to ask before renting the shop, employing staff, buying stock and opening up?

2   Imagine you're Ian's bank manager. What questions would you ask before you lent him any money?

◆   **Find a shop**
Ian had to search for a shop in the right place at the right rent.

◆   **Borrow money**
He had to borrow money from the bank to help pay the costs of setting up the business.

◆   **Find the right staff**
Ian could not be at the shop all the time, so he needed people to work for him.

◆   **Buy stock**
He had to decide exactly what people would want to buy.

◆   **Let people know about the shop**
Ian had to decide how best to spread the word about the new shop.

Once Just Micro was open …

The shop rapidly filled with customers. It provided a service that people wanted, because it was one of the few places in Sheffield where they could be sure to find the latest computer games. Ian noticed that many of the customers were expert games designers, who came into the shop to test their games on his computers.

After watching them for a while, he decided that there was a business in what they were doing. This was the beginning of Gremlin. Ian set up the company in a small office above Just Micro, employing some of those customers as games developers. The first products were early computer games such as Monty Mole, Suicide Express and Potty Pigeon. This was just the beginning of a successful future.

IN TRAY

1	Why was Just Micro a success?
2	How did careful planning contribute to this success?
3	What lessons are there for anyone setting up a business?
4	How did Ian show that he was enterprising?

Businesses make a profit in all sorts of different ways. Ian started by providing a **service** for people who wanted to buy computer games. When he founded Gremlin, he moved into designing and **manufacturing**. The people in the office design the games, and these are turned into CDs for sale in the shops.

Whatever the strategy, it all comes down to getting the right mix of people, materials, buildings and equipment in order to create a product that people want to buy.

PORTFOLIO PROMPTS

Find out about how the business you are investigating began. Was it just one person or a group? Is it part of a larger organisation?

KEY TERMS

○┉ Being **enterprising** means taking a risk by organising a business.

○┉ A **service** is provided by people. Hairdressers, estate agents and doctors all provide a service.

○┉ **Manufacturing** means using resources to make a physical product. It includes many of the things we buy, from T shirts to cars.

3 Gremlin grows

Up, up and away

The next step for Gremlin was to search for larger premises, since the business had rapidly outgrown the little office above the shop. Its first move was just down the road, to Carver House, but growth was so fast that it was soon on the lookout for something larger. The next stop was a splendid new building, which Gremlin rapidly filled to capacity.

Back in the little office above Just Micro, Ian Stewart had done everything himself. He decided what to develop, he employed staff, he did the accounts, he sold the products and did anything else that needed doing.

Ian is really a creative person, so he does some things much better than others. As the business grew, he started to employ people who were experts in particular fields – especially those which were not his speciality.

Gremlin's first shop (top); Carver House (middle); the new building (below)

IN TRAY

1 What do you think Ian employed people to do first?

2 Why is it better to employ specialists?

3 Once there were more people in the business, Ian had to be careful that everyone knew what was going on. Why?

4 Although Ian was pleased that the business was growing, why might he be unhappy about giving responsibility to other people?

In most small businesses, the owner carries out most of the tasks that need to be done. However, as the business grows it becomes harder to cope, so new people are taken on with skills that add to those of the existing staff. Here are some examples of the sorts of activity you might find in a business.

◆ A secretary might look after the office and deal with communications with people outside the business.

◆ **Production** needs to be organised and controlled. A business has to buy the materials it needs at the best price and make sure that the products will be in the shops at the right time.

- **Marketing** is important to help the business sell its products. It has to think carefully about how to package the product, what price to charge, and where to advertise and promote the product.

- Financial expertise is often brought in as it is important to control the money coming in and going out.

In a small firm, you may find just one expert in a field, but in a large business there may be whole departments.

CDs being manufactured

But what does the business do?

The simple answer is that Gremlin designs and makes computer games – but how do all these people fit together?

> *An idea is researched and developed into basic designs and scripts, then thoroughly discussed before it is turned into a story board. The design is then improved before the scripts and graphics are finalised. Depending on the game, this can involve character development, preparing film schedules, enlisting model makers and even booking celebrities.*
>
> *All through the development of every game produced by Gremlin, state-of-the-art technology is used to realise the ideas and dreams of our Creative Department, together with a professional and enthusiastic Marketing team, who bring the project to the wider world.*

IN TRAY

1   Draw a **flow chart** showing the processes involved in creating a computer game.
2   What is missing from the description above?
3   Where do you think the missing parts of the process would fit into the flow chart?

KEY TERMS

🗝 **Production** means using resources to make products.

🗝 **Marketing** consists of all the processes involved in making sure that a product is just what people want to buy.

🗝 A **flow chart** shows the way processes fit together.

Being enterprising

Organising a business, or enterprise, takes some initiative. It often results from the combination of having an idea and the ability to make things happen. Ian Stewart obviously had both. There are many sources of help for people who plan to start their own business. Banks can provide information, and the government has schemes that aim to help people get their plans off the ground. Ian has now sold Gremlin to a large games business.

PORTFOLIO PROMPTS

- Make a list of all the different activities in the business you are investigating. Who is responsible for each one?

- Draw a flow chart to show what the business does.

The marketing department

The marketing department's task is to attract visitors to the zoo from all over the country and beyond. It encourages membership of the zoo and markets the cafés, restaurants, kiosks and shops. It is also responsible for producing all literature and promoting the zoo on the television and radio.

The finance department

The finance department looks after all aspects of the financial health of the business, controlling money taken at the gates, looking after wages for staff, and producing accounts and forecasts. In this business the finance department also looks after the administration function. This is not always the case. Sometimes each function within a business will have its own administration department.

The estates department

The zoo has extensive grounds, so there is an Estates Division which is responsible for the gardens, buildings, lakes and transport around the zoo.

The education department

Chester Zoo believes it has a wonderful resource for education. The zoo's education department promotes all sorts of educational activity for every level of student, from primary school to university.

The animal department

The animal department is in charge of all animal welfare, from feeding to grooming to health. It has experts who are able to look after the animals. This department is similar to a production department in a business that makes things.

IN TRAY

1 Explain the role of each department.

2 Why does Chester Zoo need experts to work with the animals?

3 Which departments would be involved with the introduction of a new animal to the zoo? What would they have to do?

4 What do you think are the advantages of one department being in charge of all the administration?

5 What connections do you think there are between the finance department and the other departments?

What's the structure?

Many businesses organise themselves using a **hierarchical structure**, in which the people at the top have more responsibility than those further down. At the very top is one person who takes responsibility for the decisions that are made. There may also be assistants or deputies at a second level.

The heads of departments often come next. In some organisations, the heads of big departments may have a more important role in decision making than heads of small departments.

Within a department there will be a hierarchy as well. The head may have a deputy and there may be people who are responsible for specific areas.

The effectiveness of systems like this depends on people's ability to delegate. A good manager will allocate work to people who are capable of doing it well. They will then monitor the work to make sure that it is carried out.

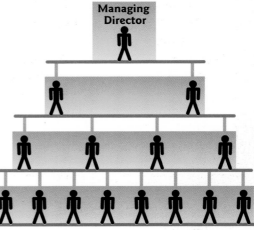

Managing Director

ACTION

Draw up an organisation chart for your school.

KEY TERM

In a **hierarchical structure** there are several layers of responsibility and departments organised by function.

10a How many layers?

OBJECTIVES

To find out why a business decided to make its organisation much simpler.

To examine how the business has become more efficient and more profitable.

A powerful solution

When Eastern Generation bought Ironbridge power station, it needed reorganising. Before it changed hands, it was organised very differently, with several **layers** of **management**. Everyone was responsible to someone else and it was difficult to get decisions made. Simple jobs were the responsibility of one person. In the maintenance department, for example, a fitter would fit a part, an electrician would mend a fuse and a mechanic would mend a machine.

All this had to change. The size of the workforce fell from 500 to 130, and those remaining were put into teams and retrained so that they became skilled at all the jobs that needed doing in their part of the organisation. This is known as **multi-skilling**. Each team has one person in charge, so all those layers of management are no longer necessary.

IN TRAY

1 How many people did the power station lose when it was reorganised?

2 Why was it important to reduce the size of the workforce?

3 Why was it difficult to work with so many layers of management?

4 What are the advantages of working in a team to get things done?

5 Why is it better for the business to work in this way?

ACTION

1 Ask members of your family if they work as part of a team. Can they find out how many layers of management there are at work?

2 Go into your local supermarket and observe the different job roles. Find out if the workers can do different jobs or whether they always stay at the same task. How many layers of management are there in the store?

PORTFOLIO PROMPTS

How many layers of management are there in the business that you are investigating? Has it changed at all?

Too many layers?

As a business grows, people are put in charge of different parts of it. This can lead to many layers of responsibilities, with decisions taking a long time to be made because everyone has to be consulted. It can be a very expensive way to run a business, but some organisations can only be run in a hierarchical way.

Communication can be difficult. If people don't know the latest news, they may become unhappy about their jobs because they feel excluded and that their views don't matter.

Many businesses have moved towards a **flat structure** organisation, with fewer layers, because they need to employ fewer people. People tend to work better because they are more involved. Training people to do a range of jobs is much more efficient, as no one is held up because the right person is not available. Teams can work well because everyone feels they are important and works hard not to let their fellow team members down.

Flatter organisations and teamworking often go hand in hand because teams allow people to take responsibility for their own work.

A matrix

Remember Future Publishing? It has developed a different sort of structure to meet the needs of the organisation. The function of the business is to create magazines. To do this effectively requires teamwork involving a range of skills. The company still needs people in overall charge of the main functional areas. Each magazine has someone who is responsible for marketing. They work for the team, but they also report to the Marketing Director. This structure is known as a matrix.

CHECKPOINT

Before

Long chain of command

After

Flatter structure

1 How many layers were there: (a) before the change of ownership? (b) after the change of ownership?

2 Explain the way people work in different organisations such as these.

3 Which structure would you prefer to work in? Why?

KEY TERMS

☞ **Management** is a term used to describe the people who organise the business at different levels.

☞ **Layer** is a level of management.

☞ **Multi-skilling** means that workers are trained to perform a number of tasks. It makes each person a flexible member of a team.

☞ A **flat structure** is one with few layers of management.

11 Who's right for the job?

OBJECTIVES

To find out how a business recruits and retains its staff, and to examine methods of selection.

Finding people

Magna Specialist Foods makes chocolate novelties. The business starts making Christmas confectionery in May and Easter eggs in September.

The company needs 150 staff all the year round, and 600 more at peak times. It must be sure to have all the staff it needs. It is easy enough to find staff who are with the company all the year round, but it is much harder to find temporary staff who have the right skills.

IN TRAY

1 Why does Magna have difficulty recruiting staff?
2 What problems does it create for a business if people are difficult to recruit?
3 Explain the advantages and disadvantages there would be for someone taking a seasonal job at Magna.

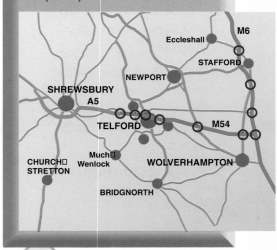

Some of Magna's chocolate novelties (above); Telford and the surrounding area (below)

Attracting and selecting

In order to choose good recruits who have the right skills for the job, Magna asks all the people who apply to work at their business to do some tests.

First, they are given a dexterity test, in which they have to use their hands and follow simple instructions. Then they are interviewed to see how well they did in their tests. Finally, they fill in a questionnaire that helps to show whether they are suitable, and acts as a double-check on the other tests.

Because there are lots of jobs around Telford, buses are provided to attract people from further afield.

IN TRAY

1 Why is dexterity important for a job in a factory?
2 Why are the interview and personality test important?
3 What is meant by 'being right for the job'?
4 Why did Sue need to advertise far afield?
5 Why did Magna offer transport?

The right people

The **human resources** department is responsible for all the people who work in a company. A key responsibility is to ensure that the business has the right staff in post.

Businesses use a variety of techniques for selecting people. Large companies will advertise nationally for some posts, while others will be filled from the local area. The nature of the interview depends on the job, but it may involve demonstrating a skill such as dexterity, working with a group or doing a presentation. Candidates will be asked to show evidence of the qualifications they have put on the application form.

Keeping people

Once the company has found new staff, it is important to keep them. Many businesses offer:

◆ a pension scheme

◆ increased holiday entitlement

◆ health care.

A candidate performs a dexterity test

CHECKPOINT

1 Why do pension schemes, increased holidays and health care encourage people to stay with a business?

2 Why is it important to keep staff once you have recruited them?

3 Can you think of other things that Magna might do to keep its staff?

People are the most valuable resource any business has, so making sure those who work in an organisation are well motivated is very important.

A human resources manager is concerned with the staff's welfare, making sure they are being treated fairly and that the work they are doing is appropriate to their training, experience and ability.

The human resources department is involved in decisions about recruitment, selection, induction, pay reviews, training, discipline, dismissal and redundancy. It is often responsible for health and safety, and monitoring changes in employment and company law.

PORTFOLIO PROMPTS

• Find out about the recruitment process in the business you are investigating.

• Draw a flow chart showing the different stages of recruitment.

ACTION

1 Choose an advertisement out of your local newspaper. Decide what you think the job requires you to do. Set up an interview between you and a classmate where he or she interviews you for the job.

2 Write a job description for a human resources manager.

KEY TERM

⌐ **Human resources** are the people who work for a business.

11a In at the deep end

Was it unfair?

Anna had recently been promoted in the human resources department. Her first task was to find out why the company was facing the threat of a case of unfair dismissal.

She knew that unfair dismissal occurs when an employee feels that the reasons given for dismissing them do not seem fair. The employee has the right to take the case to an industrial tribunal, where disputes are settled quickly and cheaply. Industrial tribunals were intended to be more informal than ordinary courts.

Melanie Brown, the person in question, had left the company two months ago. According to her manager, she had left of her own free will. Melanie had made mistakes in her work, and the manager had given her a verbal warning and a written warning that her work was unsatisfactory. If he had given her a second written warning, he would have been able to dismiss her, but she had left before this became necessary. The manager explained that he and Melanie had not really hit it off from the beginning, and he was relieved when she left.

It was now up to Anna to find out what had happened. Had it become impossible for Melanie to do her job? Was she given suitable guidance about the standards that were expected of her? Perhaps she would claim constructive dismissal, which means that she had left because it was made impossible for her to carry out her job.

Anna considered all the facts. She knew Phil Parker could be a difficult manager. She had overheard other members of his department complaining about him, but she knew very little about Melanie's work. It was now up to Anna to compile a report for her boss.

 IN TRAY

1	Why did Anna think that this was not a case of unfair dismissal?
2	Why do you think Melanie was considering bringing the case?
3	Why is work like this difficult for the human resources department?
4	Why were industrial tribunals set up?
5	Why are laws needed to protect people from being treated unfairly at work?

When considering the problem with Melanie, Anna was using the **Employment Rights Act 1996,** which sets out all the employee's rights to expect fair treatment at work. It covers pay, time off, union membership, redundancy and maternity rights, among others.

There are a number of other **Acts** that protect the employee.

◆ The **Disability Discrimination Act 1995** helps people with disabilities to lead independent lives and enjoy equal opportunities. A person is defined as disabled if he or she has a physical or mental impairment which has a long-term effect on his or her ability to carry out normal day-to-day activities.

◆ The **Sex Discrimination Act 1975** makes it unlawful to discriminate against men and women on the grounds of their sex. Anna was surprised to find out that 40 per cent of the cases of sex discrimination are brought by men.

◆ The **Race Relations Act 1976** states that it is unlawful to discriminate against a person on grounds of colour, race, nationality and ethnic or national origins.

What's the solution?

If Melanie did bring a case, Anna knew that at least there was a body that would try to mediate – the Advisory, Conciliation and Arbitration Service (ACAS). Its role is to help settle disputes before they reach the tribunal.

If a complaint does go to a tribunal, the employee is entitled to legal advice. After the hearing, the tribunal makes its decision. If this is in favour of the employee, the tribunal can order that:

◆ the employee gets the job back

◆ the employee is given another job

◆ compensation is paid.

preventing and resolving collective disputes

ACTION

Write a fact sheet explaining the main points included in the Employment, Sex, Race and Disability Acts that protect people at work.

KEY TERM

☞ An **Act** is a law which has been passed by Parliament.

IN TRAY

1 Explain the role of ACAS. Why is it helpful?

2 What can happen if the company loses the case?

3 Why is it important to have a range of laws to protect the employee?

PORTFOLIO PROMPTS

Use the newspapers to find some examples of cases taken to industrial tribunals. Which laws were being applied? Try to find at least one example of each law being applied.

12 People first

OBJECTIVES

To investigate induction and training.

To look at how Asda makes sure its staff perform effectively to achieve the business aims and objectives.

The customer is always right

Starting a new job at Asda is exciting. The company aims to make sure that new recruits understand its aims and objectives. It gives them opportunities to learn new skills and follow correct procedures.

The induction booklet says:

> Because you are the most important ingredient it is important that you know what to do and where to fit in.

The new recruits follow a 12-week training programme, which involves training sessions in a classroom learning on the sales floor. They are constantly reminded of the customer's importance.

The first day in any new job is nerve-racking, and it is important that new staff are made to feel welcome. The timetable for the first day's training at Asda is on the left.

The managers at the store work together to ensure that the first day is informative, informal and reassuring. New staff are shown a video, which demonstrates the right way to deal with customers.

Training is an ongoing process at Asda. After 12 weeks, staff have opportunities to climb a ladder of skills, gaining recognition as they become more competent and proficient in their job.

The first day's training timetable

- getting to know Asda
- working for Asda
- getting to know your store
- health and safety
- hygiene
- security
- customer service – selling with personality
- Asda's way of communicating

The Asda Way Job Ladder

- Further development
- Continuous learning
- Specialist training
- Department training
- Induction

IN TRAY

1 Explain why each section of the first day's training is important.

2 Why is training important to good customer service?

3 Why do you think Asda arranges training both in the store and in a classroom?

4 What are the advantages to Asda staff of such intensive training?

5 'Training is about continuous improvement.' Can you explain this phrase?

Initial training when a person starts a new job is called an **induction** programme. Asda has a staged induction programme that forms the first 12 weeks of training.

When training takes place in a classroom away from the workplace, it is known as **off the job training**. This kind of training is important when recruits need to learn about things such as health and safety, company policy, company aims and objectives, and the rules and regulations they have to abide by. Some of the first day of the induction programme at Asda involves off the job training.

Much of the training, however, takes place on the shop floor. This is known as **on the job training** and is very important because it enables new recruits to learn how to do the job well and practise new skills. Customer satisfaction is very important to Asda, as you can see from its mission.

The Asda mission

To be Britain's best Fresh Food and Clothing Superstore, satisfying the weekly shopping needs of ordinary working people and their families who demand value.

IN TRAY

1 What sort of skills are needed by people who work in the store to help Asda meet its mission?

2 What sort of training would help people to gain these skills?

Asda's training programme leads staff up the ladder. By undergoing training in both specific and general areas, staff can be promoted to higher levels of responsibility. All of Asda's training aims to develop each person to meet its mission and to offer every Asda employee continuous learning.

PORTFOLIO PROMPTS

Find out how training is carried out in the business that you are investigating.

ACTION

1 Write a letter to your local supermarket asking for details of its training programme for new recruits.

2 Write an induction programme for students who will be starting the GNVQ programme next year. Remember all the things you had to learn when you began.

KEY TERMS

Induction is the process of learning a new job and learning about the company. It usually starts with off the job training, and soon becomes on the job training.

Off the job training takes place away from the work environment. It is usually conducted in a training room, with a trainer giving information or teaching a new skill.

On the job training is completed while actually performing the job. It can include watching someone else at work, simply practising a skill over and over again, or doing a job while someone else is watching you to give you feedback.

13 Safe and sound

Is it safe?

Everyone at Magna Specialist Foods is responsible for health and safety.

The factory can be a dangerous place, but every measure is taken to make it safe. The floor is marked out with walkways to keep people away from the machinery. Forklift truck drivers weave in and out along these walkways all the time. They are highly trained, and are only allowed to drive the forklift if they have a certificate to prove they are competent.

It is also important that the chocolate products leaving the factory are up to the required health standards. As Magna uses food in its production process, it is essential that hygiene factors are taken into consideration. Every worker who enters the production area has to wear protective clothing and a hairnet. Among other things, workers are forbidden to wear jewellery, and beards must be covered too.

IN TRAY

1　Why are health and safety so important?

2　What does Magna do to avoid problems?

3　Magna sells its products to bigger companies. What would happen if the chocolate novelties were not up to scratch?

What's the problem?

A factory environment can be a very hazardous place. It will have machinery working at high speeds, possibly with sharp cutting equipment, and the process may be using liquids that are very hot or very cold. Floors may be slippery or sticky.

Even an office is not without its hazards. Desks and chairs may be too high or too low, and looking at a computer screen for long periods is bad for the eyes.

Because of all this, businesses have to conform to laws concerning health and safety, and any company caught ignoring them may find itself in court.

Up to scratch

Many of the staff on the shop floor at Magna are trained in health and safety. They achieve a qualification and obtain a certificate. The supervisors are also trained in first aid. They wear black hats instead of white so that they can be identified quickly if someone does have an accident.

A record of all accidents must be kept, and any accidents are reviewedto find out why they happened, and to ensure that the problem never arises again. Fortunately, Magna's accident record is very low.

IN TRAY

1   Why is it important that people are trained in health and safety matters?

2   Why must every incident or accident be investigated fully?

3   How is the business helped by looking after people in this way?

What does the law say?

The Health and Safety at Work Act of 1974 says that employers must protect the health and safety of all staff. The Act states:

◆   Firms must provide all necessary safety equipment and clothing free of charge.

◆   Employers must provide a safe working environment.

◆   All firms with five or more employees must have a written safety policy on display.

◆   Union-appointed safety representatives have the right to investigate and inspect the workplace and the causes of any accidents.

The Health and Safety Commission is responsible for employing factory inspectors, who go into factories to investigate possible breaches of the Health and Safety Act. They also offer advice and help on how safety practices might be improved.

ACTION

1   Design a poster to warn people of the dangers present in a working environment.

2   Find out which teacher at your school is responsible for health and safety. Ask him or her to tell you about what it involves. Organise a safety audit of your school.

3   Find out where you can gain qualifications in health and safety and first aid.

PORTFOLIO PROMPTS

How does the company that you are investigating deal with health and safety?

33

Go with the flow

Businesses use **flow production** when a continuous process can be used to make a product. The foil produced by Lawson Mardon is put to many uses, but it can pass through the manufacturing stages described above no matter what its purpose.

The foil is made in a continuous process, and each stage is linked to the next by a conveyor belt. This method of production is used when a large quantity of the same product is being made. All sorts of things are produced in this way. The chocolate eggs that are wrapped in the foil will be made by flow production, and so will food, and many things made out of plastic and metal. Although the machinery is often very expensive to buy, it can be used all the time so it earns its keep.

Flow production means that people can be trained for a range of jobs that are all very clear cut. The tasks stay the same, even when the product changes. In this way, people can become highly skilled at their particular task. Flow production also helps to maintain quality, because the same basic process is being used and people are applying skills to do a task that they know well.

Most of the sweets in the picture are wrapped in foil like that produced at Lawson Marsdon

Getting it right

Quality means making sure that the product meets the standards for which it is to be used. The product should be **fit for purpose** and it should always be **right first time**. There are many theories and ideas about how best to make sure a product is right first time. Lawson Mardon believes the best way to maintain its high standards is to have a programme called *The Best Way Forward*. It says:

> 'The Best Way Forward *expresses our commitment to achieving success through recognition of our people, our environment and the community in every aspect of our work.*'

Getting the product right first time also involves people thinking about the production process. If businesses are not careful, employees can become bored by their working environment.

Lawson Mardon has achieved the '**Investors in People**' award, which is a government standard that recognises that the company invests in its people through a high level of training.

INVESTORS IN PEOPLE

ACTION

What sort of things can be produced by using flow production? Can you think of any that can't?

KEY TERMS

☞ **Flow production** is the manufacture of a product in a continually moving process.

☞ '**Investors in People**' is a government programme that gives businesses a framework for staff development.

PORTFOLIO PROMPTS

Is flow production used in the business that you are investigating?

45

20 Making something special

Dreams come true

Jenny Tyler makes dreams come true. She designs and makes wedding dresses and evening wear for people who want something different.

Jenny started her business nine years ago from a room above her garage. Now she has a shop where she displays sample dresses and accessories, and a workshop above the shop where she designs and makes the dresses. She employs three people to help her make the clothes, although she still does a lot of the work herself.

Each dress is crafted carefully by Jenny and her team. Jenny draws the design and ascertains the client's budget, which in turn influences the choice of fabric and accessories. The average price of a dress is £1,300. Jenny always asks for a deposit of a third of the price to cover the cost of buying fabric and the first part of making up the dress. Jenny emphasises that if she didn't take this much deposit, she would be out of pocket buying the fabric and starting the work.

Jenny may be working on up to ten dresses at a time, but each dress can take up to three months to make. The first part of the process is making the dress in cotton to make sure it fits. Then it is made in its final fabric. There is a first and second 'silk' fitting, and then a final fitting. Some of the garments are hand-painted or hand-embroidered, and each one is unique.

Jenny has customers all over the country. Her dresses are often photographed and featured in magazines, and she has won several awards for her work.

Making a wedding dress in the workshop

IN TRAY

1   Why do Jenny's dresses have to be made individually?

2   How can Jenny make ten dresses at a time?

3   Explain why the dresses could not be made by flow production.

4   Is it more or less expensive to produce things this way? Why?

Some of Jenny Tyler's unique designs

Jenny's business is an example of **job production**, which means that each item or unit is made individually, usually with one person working on it from start to finish. It is an important process in the manufacture of such items as celebration cakes, hand-made furniture and tailor-made suits. It is also very expensive, because it takes a long time to make one item.

Job production is a traditional method of production and is still important for people who want something special or unique. Craftspeople using this method of production are difficult to find because they need to be very skilled at what they do, and this takes a long time to learn. Few people are prepared to spend many years learning such specialised skills, so it is up to people like Jenny Tyler to keep traditional methods of production alive.

ACTION

Look in the *Yellow Pages* to find out if there is a local craftsperson working in your area creating unique or different items. Write them a letter asking if you can have a demonstration of what they do. If possible, take photographs of the expert at work.

CHECKPOINT

1 Make a list of the advantages and disadvantages of job production.

2 How many things can you think of that are likely to be made by job production? Make a list.

KEY TERM

⚷ **Job production** is used to make products that need individual attention.

5 Do you think that people enjoy working in this environment?

6 Why is it important for Jenny to take a large deposit before she starts?

7 What factors helped Jenny to make a success of her business?

8 Would it be easy for Jenny to expand her business?

PORTFOLIO PROMPTS

Is job production used in the business that you are investigating?

21 A cut above

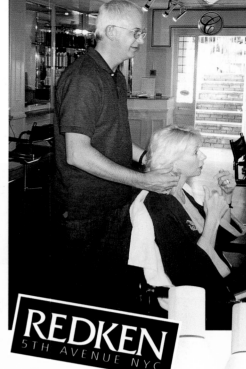

Producing a new look

Steve Chester runs his own hairdressing salon. His business has grown over many years, developing a loyal customer base by providing a high-quality service at a fair price. He has never advertised his salon, relying on his reputation to sell his services.

Steve knows that paying wages to his staff is his biggest cost, but he also realises that they are vital to the success of his business. He employs experienced stylists as well as taking on trainees who have just left school. Because Steve is a qualified training instructor, he trains all his staff at the salon. As his trainees become more proficient, they can train new recruits. Trainees are trained by part-qualified staff, who are in turn trained by qualified staff. Sometimes people choose to specialise, for example becoming a technician in colour, cut or perms. Even experienced and expert staff have to continue to train.

Getting the balance right between the number of staff he has and the number of people wanting to book a hair appointment is tricky. Steve does not want to have people hanging around doing nothing, nor does he want to keep his customers waiting because he has too few staff.

Hairdressers have other resources to think about as well as staff: the products they use to colour hair, the shampoos, conditioners, perm solutions, special treatments, hairsprays and gels. Buying good quality products at a fair price is important to produce the right finish for every customer. It is also essential to have enough stock of each item so that the customer won't be disappointed or dissatisfied. Hairdressers need to buy towels and have them laundered every day. They need equipment to dry, shape and style the hair.

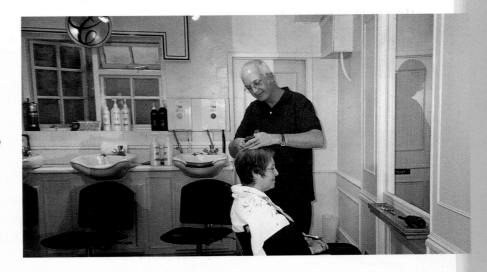

Steve buys most of the things he needs from a wholesaler who specialises in selling to hairdressing salons. However, recently he has started to use Redken products and to sell them to his customers as well. He believes the product has a good reputation and looks stylish on display. Steve is careful about his costs, making sure he takes advantage of special offers and discounts.

IN TRAY

1   Make a list of the resources that are used by a hairdressing business.

2   Why is training so important in Steve's business?

3   Why is it a good idea for Steve to encourage staff who show they have talent?

4   How does Steve make a profit?

5   How does Steve market his business?

6   What helps to make a business that provides a service successful?

Selling a service

Services come in all shapes and sizes. The local gym provides a service, so does the car showroom and the corner shop. Solicitors, schools and bus companies are all in the same category.

Even though service industries do not provide something that you can carry away, they still need resources. In the service sector, people are the main resource of many businesses, and staff must have the right skills and be trained to provide an efficient service.

An office or shop is often essential, as it provides a location for the business. It will, of course, need heat and light in order to work effectively. Computers and other kinds of equipment, as well as the power to run them, are also among the resources that the business will have to pay for.

Whatever the service, the business will aim to sell it at a profit. It will therefore be careful to ensure that the service's selling price is above its cost of production.

CHECKPOINT

Choose two service industries and make a list of the resources that are needed to run them.

ACTION

1   Do a survey of the cost of different hairdressing salons in your area. How far does cost relate to the kind of customer the salon aims to attract?

2   Do a survey of your classmates. Ask them where they go to have their hair cut, why they go there and what they pay.

PORTFOLIO PROMPTS

If the business that you are investigating provides a service, draw a flow chart to show the resources that it uses in the process.

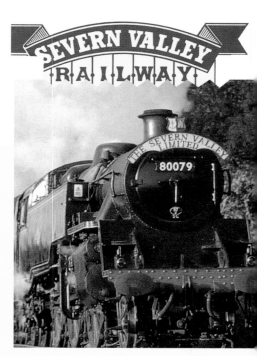

21a Steaming ahead

OBJECTIVES

To find out what businesses have to do to perform effectively when providing a service or making a product.

On the fast track

Steam has a magnetic attraction for many people. The Severn Valley Railway, with its beautifully restored stations and steam locomotives, raises memories of yesteryear.

Although many of its staff are volunteers, the company must make a profit in order to develop. To do this it must attract more visitors and increase turnover.

Severn Valley Railway is really many businesses rolled into one.

◆ It offers memorable train journeys.

◆ It buys, renovates and maintains locomotives.

◆ Each station provides catering services offering home-made sandwiches, snacks and cakes.

◆ Two stations have real ale pubs.

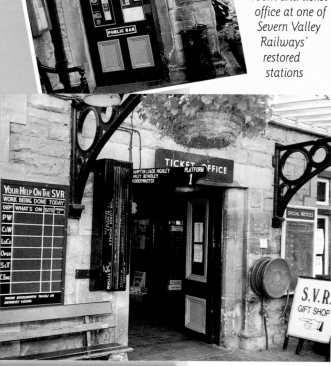

A refreshment room and ticket office at one of Severn Valley Railways' restored stations

IN TRAY

1 What are the main aims of the Severn Valley Railway company?

2 For each part of the business, make a list of the resources needed to run successfully.

3 Why are volunteers important to the business?

4 What might the company do to meet its objectives of growth?

5 Why do you think the Severn Valley Railway is so important to the town where it is based?

Rising to the challenge

Every business that wants to improve has to ask itself some questions. Two important ones are:

◆ Are we achieving our objectives?

◆ How can we improve our performance?

To answer these questions, a business must try to become more effective. It can do this is by **adding value**, which means that it looks for ways to increase the value it can achieve from the resources it uses.

People buy lettuces for about 50p each. They also buy bags of mixed lettuce that is washed and ready to use at a price of £1.50 or more. Supermarkets have added value to the product. By preparing the salad and putting it in a bag, they have added little to the cost, but have developed a product for which people are prepared to pay a higher price.

Quality can also lead to improvement. The quality of a product is crucial. A cheap T-shirt will obviously not be of the same quality as an expensive one, but it must at least meet the expectations of the customer.

Many businesses also look for quality in the way the organisation is run. The British Standards Institute offers a quality standard, ISO 9000, which a business can apply for. The whole business has to be audited to demonstrate that quality is important in everything it does.

Being competitive

If a business's objective is to increase its profit, it must persuade people to buy more of its products or find ways of making them more cheaply. In other words, it must become more competitive. Adding value and quality are both important in this process.

Businesses constantly look for ways to reduce costs, for example by buying resources more cheaply or making the production process more efficient.

Getting better

Severn Valley Railway keeps its eye on these questions all the time and can report:

- a successful marketing and media campaign
- passengers up by 8.4 per cent
- a high level of customer satisfaction
- turnover exceeding £3 million, up by 5.4 per cent
- a serious investment in catering facilities at the stations and on board the trains
- increased expenditure on locomotive maintenance

IN TRAY

1 How does Severn Valley Railway add value?

2 How might it improve quality?

3 Draw a flow chart to show how the company has achieved its objectives.

4 How does the achievement of these objectives help the company to improve in future?

CHECKPOINT

Look at a range of personal stereos, or other products that you know about, and explain how the models add value. Do new features mean that the company can charge a higher price?

ACTION

Find out how your school measures quality.

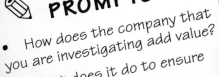

PORTFOLIO PROMPTS

- How does the company that you are investigating add value?
- What does it do to ensure quality?
- Find out whether the business has set itself targets and whether it has achieved them.

KEY TERMS

⊙—π **Added value** is the difference between the costs of inputs into the product and the price that customers are prepared to pay.

⊙—π **Quality** in a product means that it at least reaches customers' expectations. It is also used to measure how effectively a business is run.

22 What is marketing about?

Lizard Lighthouse, Cornwall

Attracting trippers

Have you ever visited a castle, stately home or beach, or walked along a spectacular coastal path? If you have, there's a strong possibility that it belongs to the National Trust, a voluntary organisation that does not trade for profit. Its aim is to buy and preserve beautiful and historic sites for the benefit of everyone. It is a large organisation with a turnover from sales of over £160 million a year. It employs over 3,000 permanent staff, 4,000 seasonal staff and has 38,000 volunteers.

The Trust needs to raise income from members and visitors so that it can look after its properties and buy new ones. It relies heavily on marketing to meet its aims and spends about £7 million a year on publicity. Its marketing targets include:

◆ getting 12 million paying visits in the year 2000

◆ providing a worthwhile experience for its customers

◆ achieving annual income targets

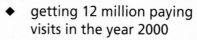

Some of the National Trust's resources

◆ over 390 houses, farms, churches and gardens

◆ 19 castles

◆ 49 industrial monuments

◆ many areas of coastline and countryside

Bodmin Castle

IN TRAY

1 Why does the National Trust do so much marketing?

2 Why does it set itself marketing targets?

3 Which targets are financial and which one is not?

4 What sort of things would you suggest that the National Trust does in order to achieve its targets?

5 What costs will the Trust have to meet if it carries out the activities you suggest?

What is marketing?

Marketing is an activity that is carried out by almost all businesses. It involves:

- finding out what people want
- providing what they want
- letting them know where and how to buy the product or service

Whatever the style of marketing, the objective is the same – the business wants to increase or at least maintain sales. The way this works in different organisations will vary, as you can see from the two pieces of evidence here. Both businesses have different objectives, and each is developing a marketing plan to achieve them.

We're all going to the zoo?

Chester Zoo has suffered a steady decline in visitors, just like many other zoos across the country. There are so many competing attractions that zoos have to work hard to attract customers.

Chester Zoo has five simple and clear marketing objectives:

- to encourage customers to return
- to get new visitors
- to have an even spread of visitors over the whole season
- to raise awareness of the zoo's work in conservation
- to sell lots of food, drink and souvenirs make a good profit and leave customers feeling they had value for money

Where does marketing start?

Although the importance of marketing varies in different businesses, any business that ignores marketing altogether does so at its peril. Marketing does not come cheap and requires a great deal of planning in order to be effective.

The first stage is to work out what information is needed and then to collect it. Marketing decisions should be made after considering all the information that can be gathered about the people the business is trying to persuade. It's also essential to know what the competitors are up to.

The decisions will relate to promotion and sales, since time, people and resources need to be set aside to carry out these activities. Marketing decisions also affect other areas of the business, such as production and finance. As it is mostly designed to bring in more money, marketing must be related to the overall business aims.

IN TRAY

1 Why do you think Chester Zoo wants to have an even spread of visitors throughout the year?

2 How can it attract new customers?

3 In what ways are Chester Zoo's targets similar to those of the National Trust?

ACTION

Chester Zoo has decided to increase food and drink sales. What will the business need to consider if it is to meet this aim? You may wish to look up Chester Zoo's website.

23 What do the customers want?

OBJECTIVES

To explore the different ways that businesses find out what potential customers want.

Finding out

The National Trust carries out **market research** regularly to help meet marketing targets. The marketing department wants to know:

- who are its visitors?
- how do they find out about the attractions?
- did they enjoy their visit?
- how much did they spend?

This information is gathered nationally and locally through questionnaires, member surveys, counting numbers through entrances, and testing opinions of specially invited groups of people. Questionnaires used by individual properties ask similar questions, so the results can be grouped.

Membership of the National Trust, 1994–9

Year	Members (millions)
1994	2.2
1995	2.32
1996	2.29
1997	2.4
1998	2.49
1999	2.59

IN TRAY

1 Why does the National Trust need to collect marketing information regularly?

2 Why does collecting information through questionnaires cost more than counting people through entrances?

3 Why are questionnaires used?

Researching the market

Market research allows a business to recognise what customers want and provides an opportunity for the business to meet these needs. Finding out the right information involves a range of methods.

The National Trust's marketing team already has information about the number of visitors to its properties in the past, including when they went and how much they spent. It can also use published information, such as collecting competitors' brochures or using general statistics. This research is often known as desk research, or **secondary research**, since the information already exists somewhere.

However, it is often necessary for the National Trust to find out more specific information, such as how far visitors have travelled, how much

THE NATIONAL TRUST

From this research, it has become clear that 'word of mouth' is the best way of encouraging visitors to its properties. The Trust has therefore placed greater importance on customer care, including providing better facilities and a warmer welcome at each property.

Membership has been increasing steadily, but the Trust is always looking to grow more quickly.

4 What is the advantage of grouping the results of surveys?

5 How has the information collected been useful?

they enjoyed their visit and what would make it better. Gathering this information is called **primary research**, which means collecting original information. This can often be expensive.

Analysing market research data involves looking for trends and groups of information.

Who is going to the zoo?

Zoos all use market research to collect information about their customers. By analysing the information collected, they can aim marketing at the likely group of customers.

Look at the information collected by Chester Zoo.

Have you been to the zoo since you were 10? Did your parents or grandparents take you? The next time you are likely to go to the zoo will be as an adult taking your own children. How do zoos know this? The marketing department at Chester Zoo collects information by:

◆ yearly visitor surveys carried out by the zoo staff

◆ reading existing published information

◆ all the staff watching and listening to customers

CHECKPOINT

1 Which is the cheapest method of research?

2 Which is likely to give the least relevant information?

3 Why do businesses spend money on market research?

ACTION

Can market research be more accurate? Find out people's opinions about your school. Who should you ask? How many people do you need to ask, and what questions should you put to them?

PORTFOLIO PROMPTS

What sort of market research is carried out by the business that you are investigating?

KEY TERMS

○┉ **Market research** is used to find out about what customers want and what competitors are doing.

○┉ **Primary research** involves first-hand investigations.

○┉ **Secondary research** uses data that have been collected by others and can be found in books and reports or on the web.

24 What's in a survey?

OBJECTIVES

To learn about how to carry out a survey.

Finding out

Chester Zoo conducts a survey every year. The zoo pays a specialist market research business to make up a questionnaire and analyse the results. The zoo's marketing staff then carry out the interviews by selecting summer visitors at random.

Carrying out market research

Chester Zoo groups the questions into three broad areas. First are questions about its customers: the zoo wants to know their ages, why they decided to visit the zoo, how long they spent there, when they arrived, how they got there and where they came from.

The second group of questions shows how effective its marketing is. An example of what the marketing team asks is shown right.

The third set of questions asks for customers' views or opinions. Some of the questions asked are shown on the left.

Chester Zoo

1 Have you seen or heard any advertising for the zoo lately?

◆ Yes:	54%

2 Where did you see or hear it? (could be more than one)

◆ TV	39%
◆ Newspaper	10%
◆ Radio	3%
◆ Poster	1%
◆ Other, e.g. leaflet, on a bus	4%

Chester Zoo

What do you most like about the zoo?

What is your favourite animal?

What do you like least?

How could the zoo be improved?

Do you get good value for the admission charge?

◆ Extremely good	10%
◆ Very good	58%
◆ Fairly good	30%
◆ Not very good	1%
◆ Not at all	0%
◆ Don't know	0%

IN TRAY

I	Why use a market research organisation to make up and analyse the questions?
2	Why does the zoo conduct a survey every year?
3	How would you phrase the questions that are about the zoo's customers?
4	Which of the sample questions ask the person interviewed to choose an answer?

Asking the right questions

Finding out new information through a questionnaire is primary research. The questionnaire needs to be carefully planned to give the information you want.

Questionnaires often start with **closed questions**, which give a choice of answers. The information collected is limited, but it is easy to collect and sort. Questions with no preset answers are **open-ended** and are often used to find out people's views. The information they give is more difficult to collate.

It would be expensive and impossible to ask every customer, but enough people need to be questioned to make the results valid. It is also important to ask the right people, and there are different ways of choosing them.

◆ At random, so that everyone has an equal chance of being questioned.

◆ Grouping people according to age, gender or income and asking a set number of people from each group.

◆ Targeting one of these groups, for instance a business that organises children's parties would target parents with young children.

Top tips

1 Try out the questionnaire on a few people first before making it final.

2 Be polite when asking questions. Practise on your friends.

3 Check to see if the questions will give you the information you want.

4 Don't make the questionnaire too long.

5 Decide on how you are going to choose the right people to ask.

6 Decide how many people you will need to ask.

7 Make the questionnaire easy to use.

8 Postal responses are poor, so it's much better to ask questions face to face.

9 Avoid leading questions, such as 'We think our product is great, don't you?'

10 Try to get information from other sources to help confirm the accuracy of your results.

How do surveys help?

Once the information has been sorted, it can be used to help the business monitor its targets and make decisions. The marketing team will use the information to produce a report or a marketing plan. This will be presented to senior managers from other functional areas, who will discuss its implications for their area. For example, the marketing department at the zoo recognised a need to improve catering, but this also had an effect on the human resources and finance departments.

ACTION

Conduct a survey on cans of soft drinks targeting
(a) parents and
(b) 14–16-year-olds.

KEY TERMS

🔑 **Closed questions** need a short, straightforward answer, and the results are easy to collate.

🔑 **Open-ended questions** are used when the researcher is looking for in-depth answers about people's point of view. They are difficult to collate, but give detailed information.

25 Sales, sales and more sales

OBJECTIVES

To learn about how and why a business tries to increase sales.

Making plans

Money from sales is Chester Zoo's lifeblood, and without it the zoo wouldn't survive. It also needs sales in order to invest in new facilities such as the 'Islands in Danger' development. Why does it need to develop? One reason is to keep up with new conservation and animal welfare methods. Another is to keep ahead of the **competition**, such as the nearby Blue Planet aquarium.

Marketing is important for the zoo. Its Marketing Manager, Chris Vere, is in charge of over 30 staff, including those looking after functions, catering and retailing.

Two of Chester Zoo's marketing objectives were to increase visitors and have a more even spread of visits across the season. They were going to be difficult objectives to meet, as tourism had been flat that year, and there was now real competition from the new £13 million Blue Planet aquarium just 3 miles away.

Chris and his team of senior managers had many meetings to decide on a marketing plan aimed at attracting new visitors and persuading people to make two trips to the zoo each year. Two senior managers visited other leading tourist sites such as Disney's Animal World in Florida, and came back with some new ideas for **promotion**. Research had shown that the zoo's strength was its great value for money, so this was the message that had to be brought more effectively to public attention.

IN TRAY

1 Why might a loss in sales affect conservation work?

2 In what other ways would the zoo be affected?

3 Why do you think the marketing department organised itself into sales, catering and retailing?

4 What other ways might the staff have been organised?

5 Why spend money sending managers out to look at other tourist sites?

6 The entry fee for the zoo is higher than Blue Planet. How might the zoo justify this?

The decisions

- Speed up improvements to the zoo's facilities.
- Design better education packages to attract school visits out of season.
- Increase television advertising during the early summer within 50 miles of the zoo.
- Offer free entrance coupons in newspapers and zoo leaflets.
- Develop theme events such as Christmas lunches.
- Promote use of the zoo for conferences and birthday parties.
- Make more use of the Noah's Ark float at summer shows and events in the region.

How successful was Chester Zoo?

Visitors increased by 11%, reaching 921,000.

Over 50,000 free entrance coupons claimed from local newspapers.

Over 2,000 claimed from Chester Zoo News.

Over 4,000 claimed from zoo leaflets.

The coupon campaign produced about 90,000 extra visitors.

The zoo had a surplus after costs of £1.8 million. This was the best result for 20 years.

IN TRAY

1 Which of the marketing actions are likely to:
   (a) increase the number of new visitors?
   (b) encourage visitors to return?
   (c) spread visits throughout the year?

2 What staffing problem might there be in increasing the use of the Noah's Ark float?

3 Look at the photographs and map to help you describe the other **promotion** methods.

4 Which was the most effective way of promoting the coupons? Why is it important to have accurate information about where the coupons came from?

5 How did collecting this information contribute to the zoo's objectives?

Meeting objectives

Chester Zoo more than met its objectives through its marketing activities. When making plans of this sort, a business must examine its aims and objectives and work out the best way to achieve them. Many businesses aim to increase sales, and the marketing department must coordinate all the activities that contribute to achieving this aim.

ACTION

Look up Chester Zoo on the Internet and discover in what ways the zoo uses it to help achieve its marketing objectives.

PORTFOLIO PROMPTS

What promotional activities are used by the business that you are investigating? Why?

26 Have you been Tango'd?

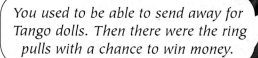

OBJECTIVES

To learn about different ways of promoting the same product and how you can research this.

I've been Tango'd

Tango products are aimed at people of your age. That's the opinion of 15-year-old Jason Pope.

> *In my opinion it appeals to everyone who is a bit wacky.*

> *There's loads of promotional stuff, too. I've heard it on the radio and seen the TV ads. I've even seen it at the side of pitches when I'm watching football on TV.*

> *I associate Tango with fun.*

> *You used to be able to send away for Tango dolls. Then there were the ring pulls with a chance to win money.*

> *Those adverts really make you look – they're, like, eye-catching. They make you think about things. They are strange, dodgy, and weird. The punchline for a series of ads is always the same, but they change the stories all the time.*

> *You can buy Tango everywhere – shops, vending machines, trains, cafés, supermarkets. It varies in price depending on where you buy it.*

Jason noted down just where he'd come across Tango in one weekend.

- At newsagents in crates.
- Two different adverts on TV.
- On sale at a food stand at a steam festival.
- Vending machine at a sports centre.
- Eye-level display in a petrol station.

IN TRAY

1. What is Tango's current **slogan** and what did it use to be?
2. Why does it change the adverts regularly?
3. What special promotions has Tango made?
4. What image is Tango trying to project? Why?
5. What other products have an image of their own?
6. How many opportunities did Jason have to buy a Tango over the weekend? Why does it vary in price so much?

Tangoing

IN TRAY

1 Where is Tango promoted?

2 Why does Tango spend so much on promoting its product?

3 Use the rest of the page to find out how departments other than the marketing department contribute to the promotion of Tango.

Promoting the product

So many soft drinks are available that Tango's marketing team needed something to make the product stand out from its competitors. It believes it has a strong image and a great slogan, and uses television and radio advertising to spread its message. The adverts are put on at times when the target audience is listening.

Many consumers buy a soft drink on impulse, and often haven't decided what to buy until the last moment. Some of the pictures show promotion at the place where the product is purchased. This **point of sales promotion** can be very effective in attracting the impulse buyer.

By spending money on promotion, Tango's marketing team has raised **brand awareness**. Do you think it has been successful?

Promotion doesn't happen on its own. Whether the activities are aimed at Tango or Chester Zoo, they require considerable planning, research and organisation. The amount to be spent must be agreed with the finance department, and production, distribution and promotion have to be coordinated. It's no good having a great promotion if you are unable to get the products to the customer. Imagine going to a vending machine or to a corner shop and not being able to get the soft drink you want. Not only is this lost sales, but it will test your **brand loyalty** if it happens more than once. The product has to be right, too. To reduce the risk of failure a business will research this by consulting customers and running test trials.

ACTION

Work out a promotional campaign for a soft drink. Explain why you have used each part of the campaign. Why is it different from the activities carried out by Chester Zoo?

KEY TERMS

🔑 A **slogan** is a catchy phrase used in adverts.

🔑 **Point of sales promotion** is how the product is promoted at the place where it is sold.

🔑 **Brand awareness** is of interest to businesses because it shows how many people know about their product.

🔑 **Brand loyalty** means customers prefer to buy one product rather than a close competitor's.

27 Bringing it all together

Things to do

Arrange for a licence to run the event.

Work out a budget, pricing and demand.

Sort out promotion methods.

Design and print leaflets.

Distribute leaflets.

Organise and start ticket sales.

Let out concessions for food and drink.

Organise volunteer stewards for the night.

Appoint temporary staff to manage the stage.

Hire lighting, toilets, car parking assistants.

Meet health and safety, police, fire brigade and environmental health organisations.

Discuss a contingency plan for emergencies.

The product

Once a year, thousands of people flock to the National Trust's Dyrham Park, a large house with extensive grounds in south-west England, for two evenings of musical events. It's aimed at those over 30 and their families, so the music must appeal to a range of people. Jools Holland was the main artist for one evening.

The reason

After paying out all the costs, the money left over from sales is used to maintain and develop National Trust properties and sites. It also raises public awareness of the property and will increase normal visits.

The team and the organisation

A weekend's event takes a year to organise and involves people from different departments. As soon as one event has finished, planning for the next begins. The project team, which includes box office staff from the National Trust Regional Office some 40 miles away, the property manager and his assistant, meets to discuss the next event. A list of bands is ranked, agents are contacted and bookings are made. Then there are so many things to organise.

The marketing mix

◆ **Setting the price**

The box office manager and the team have to decide what to charge for each evening's event. They have to consider the costs, how many people are likely to attend, and what they are prepared to pay. Any business must look carefully at the price it sets. If it is too high, few people will buy. If it is too low, it is missing an opportunity to increase its profits.

◆ **Creating the product**

The team's product is an open-air musical evening. All businesses have a product to sell, whether it is a service or a physical product, which must be carefully considered so that it meets the needs of the customer. The National Trust team had to think carefully about which bands to book for the events. If it got it wrong, few people would want to attend.

PORTFOLIO PROMPTS

What is the marketing mix for a product sold by the business that you are investigating?

Thousands of people come to the National Trust's annual musical event at Dyrham Park

The team members have many other tasks to perform and are brought together for this project, so the lines of communication between them have to be clear and each person must know what is happening. They use the phone often, as well as fax and e-mail, which are essential when documents need to be sent. Of course, they have regular meetings to monitor progress and sort out problems. The three work well as a team, each having their own qualities and skills.

IN TRAY

1 What is the purpose of running the event?

2 Who is the target audience? Why has the National Trust chosen this group?

3 Why is it important to have effective communication?

4 Which jobs would be the responsibility of the box office, and which are likely to be divided between the property manager and his assistant?

5 Which other departments will be involved?

◆ **Choosing the place**
This event takes place in the grounds of the house. In marketing terms, 'place' refers to the ways in which the product reaches the customer.

◆ **Selecting promotion**
Leaflets, posters and point of sales promotion with large boards by the entrance are used. However, the event itself and customer care are all types of promotion. If these are good one year, people will come again and tell their friends. Almost all businesses use promotional activities, from printing leaflets for local distribution to extensive national campaigns.

CHECKPOINT

Choose a product which has extensive marketing and explain the marketing mix that is being used.

KEY TERMS

⚷ The **marketing mix** is the combination of strategies businesses use for persuading people to buy a product.

⚷ **Price** must be set at a level that people are prepared to pay.

⚷ **Product** is the most important part of the mix. It must meet customer needs.

⚷ **Place** refers to how the product is distributed to the customer.

28 Why is the customer always right?

Getting it right

WHSmith knows how important it is to keep its customers happy. As customers, we have a lot of power: if we do not like the service we receive, we can always go somewhere else. This is especially true of a business like WHSmith, which is in a very competitive market with many other businesses selling similar products.

In order to be a leader, WHSmith is constantly looking for ways to improve on the quality of service that it provides. Staying at the top is all about paying attention to detail. Customers increasingly expect to buy what they want immediately, from staff who are friendly and courteous, and to pay a fair price and have plenty of choice.

WHSmith sets standards for **customer care**. This process is known as benchmarking. These benchmarks are based on best practice, which is developed through market research and by observing the activities of other businesses. All this information is pooled in order to develop a set of standards that staff must achieve.

IN TRAY

1 Why is customer service so important to business?

2 What do you think customer service means for staff working at WHSmith?

3 Why is benchmarking important to businesses that are trying to achieve a high level of customer satisfaction?

4 Why is it important for the business to be on the lookout for ways to improve?

What is good service?

There are many different ways in which a business can provide satisfaction to its customers. The customer service diagram shows some of the ways.

Information
Making the customer feel good
After-sales Advice
Point of sale
Customer Care
Customer service
Dealing with complaints
Being fair about price
Distributing the product
Having the right stock

A business must monitor customer satisfaction to make sure that it is achieving the standards it has set. There are many ways a business might do this.

- ◆ Ask customers to complete a questionnaire about the service they have received.

- ◆ Analyse sales figures to see how many customers have used its service.

- ◆ Employ outside people as 'mystery customers' to observe how the staff are performing.

Raising standards

WHSmith has worked hard to be at the top of the ladder for good customer service. It was the first retailer to achieve the 'Investors in People' award. This shows that an organisation makes sure its employees have the right training to achieve its aims and objectives. WHSmith wants to be the best in the field and to achieve this through excellent customer care. It is important that staff are trained effectively to enable it to meet this aim.

INVESTORS IN PEOPLE

'Investors in People' is a programme which gives a framework for staff development. Many businesses now have the 'Investors in People' award, which means they have invested in training and developing their staff to meet their aims and objectives. When a company has met all the requirements, it can display the 'Investors in People' kitemark. Achievement of the standard brings advantages to a business. New employees will be attracted to a company that has proved that it invests in its people, while well-trained and well-informed staff will be motivated to provide the best possible service.

IN TRAY

1 What is 'Investors in People'?

2 Why does 'Investors in People' help a business to be more efficient?

3 Why might holding the 'Investors in People' award attract customers?

ACTION

Do a survey of your local shops. How many retailers have a customer service desk? How many have a written statement about refunds and exchanges? How many have achieved an award for good customer service or staff training?

PORTFOLIO PROMPTS

- Identify the range of customer services in the business that you are investigating.

- Identify what is considered best practice. Does the business match up? How might it improve? How does it contribute to the aims of the business?

KEY TERM

⊙━ **Customer care** means thinking about the needs of the customer in every part of the business. By doing this, a business tries to ensure that customers return and the business has a good reputation.

29 Who needs help?

What do customers want?

WHSmith believes that it is essential that customers trust the staff in the stores and feel confident they have been given reliable advice.

Staff have to deal with a wide range of questions, from location of stock to those requiring expert knowledge of particular products. They are trained in how best to serve the customer while they are on the job, and sometimes in training sessions off the job with their managers. Each new recruit goes through an induction programme, which emphasises the importance of the customer to the business.

IN TRAY

1 Why is customer service so important to WHSmith?

2 What are the different methods of training used to deliver good customer practice? Why do you think the company uses both methods?

3 What do you think WHSmith's customers want?

ACTION

1 Prepare a training session for the rest of your class explaining the importance of good customer service and giving good and accurate advice.

2 Observe the staff in retail organisations in your locality. How do they treat their customers? Visit different shops and compare the service given by staff.

WHSmith asks its staff to put themselves in the customers' shoes in the following situations ...

- being shown the location of a product
- in a queue
- talking to staff
- making a specific enquiry

Its booklet uses slogans to make staff think about giving advice ...

- Am I concerned with getting what I want, or am I trying to help my customer get what they want?

- It's not just what you do, it's the way that you do it.

- Customers love to buy – they hate to be sold at.

- WHSmith is not about hard sell. It is about having the skills and ability to help customers get what they want.

PORTFOLIO PROMPTS

Find out how the business that you are investigating gives advice. Could it do better?

Good advice about customer care

Customer care takes place in different ways in different organisations, and all businesses need to pay constant attention to it. A company that makes car parts, a mail-order company and a hairdresser need to think carefully about what giving advice means in their situation. The following checklist is useful for all of them.

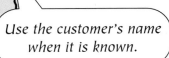

Greet customers with a smile.

Use the customer's name when it is known.

Never say no – recommend alternatives when a customer's request is not available.

Listen carefully to understand the customer's needs.

Be approachable, friendly and courteous at all times.

Respond quickly and positively to customer questions and queries.

Be able to locate the products a customer wants.

Look for, recognise and act upon a customer's need for help.

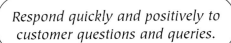

Ensure customers are made to feel important.

The booklet gives practical advice on dealing with customers ...

- Whatever you are doing, make sure you pay attention to keeping queues to a minimum.

- Always take customers to the product, never just point at it.

- Talk in a language that the customer will understand, and never use jargon.

- Always be on the lookout to see how you can improve customer service.

IN TRAY

1 What four situations has the company selected to focus on? Why do you think that these four are important?

2 Take each one and use the information to give advice to staff on providing advice or information.

3 How would you help a member of staff who was not providing a good service?

Who needs people?

As computers become more sophisticated, many tasks that used to take hours can now be done in seconds by a machine. From the previous pages, you will have seen that it is impossible to separate communications and computers.

All departments use computers now, as the quotes opposite suggest. They speed up:

◆ the work of the department

◆ communication between departments

◆ communication with the outside world

Computers are constantly changing the way that people work as their ability to communicate with each other and the outside world develops.

They also help businesses to produce sophisticated presentations, which help persuade people to buy their products or convince managers to develop a new product.

Making connections

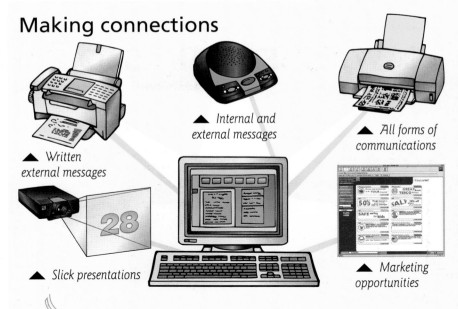

▲ Written external messages

▲ Internal and external messages

▲ All forms of communications

▲ Slick presentations

▲ Marketing opportunities

IN TRAY

1 How do computers make communication faster? Use the last four pages to help you decide.

2 How do they make communication more effective?

3 Why can a business not ignore the changes that computers bring?

Modem mobility

Modems link computers to the telephone system, which means that they can dial up the Internet and access e-mail, fax and data collection facilities. This opens up many opportunities to businesses, which are looking for ways to talk to staff, suppliers and customers. You don't even have to be in the office to receive messages. Modern technology goes with you.

◆ Mobile phones make people accessible almost anywhere. They also work as computer connections.

◆ Notebook computers are so light that they can be taken anywhere. They can be connected to the telephone system, so people can receive and send faxes, e-mails and dial up the Internet.

◆ Voice mail enables messages to be downloaded from far-flung places.

PORTFOLIO PROMPTS

• How do computers assist in the communication systems in the business you are investigating?

• Are any new processes being introduced?

1 What's it all about?

The business mix

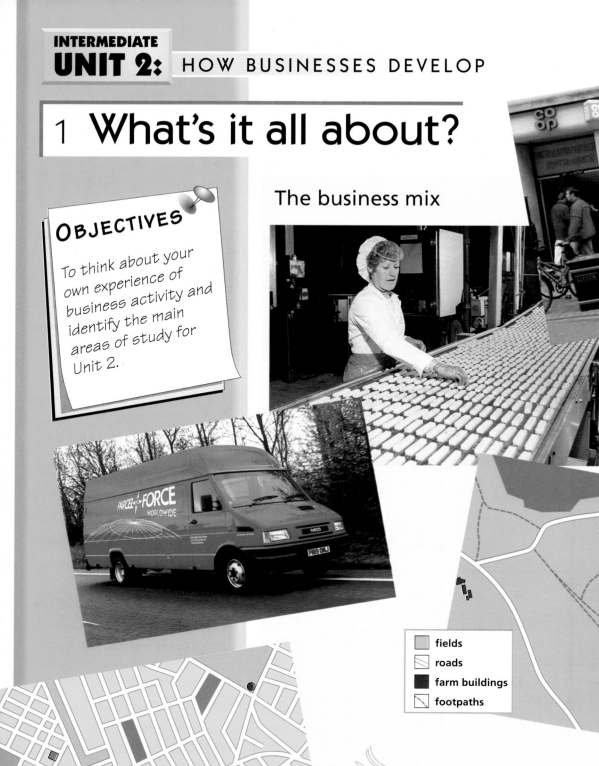

OBJECTIVES

To think about your own experience of business activity and identify the main areas of study for Unit 2.

fields
roads
farm buildings
footpaths

buildings
business areas
roads
parks

IN TRAY

1   What sorts of businesses can you see in the pictures?
2   What differences are there between them?
3   What differences are there between the areas shown in the maps?
4   Why might the businesses be different in the two areas?
5   What differences are there between the high street in the picture and a big city high street?

ACTION

1 Write down five different business activities you have seen on your way from home to school or college.

2 What do these businesses make or provide?

3 Who owns these businesses?

4 Are there any businesses that are special to your local area?

5 Who do you think makes the big decisions in these businesses?

6 How have these business activities changed over the last ten years?

All about business

You may already know some of the answers to the questions in the Action box. It's not surprising that you'll know more about some local businesses than others.

Some business activity is obvious to everyone – a garage repairs cars, a shop sells trainers, a factory turns out packets of fish fingers. Other activities are more difficult to identify – for example, a business that makes machinery for other businesses, or the sorting that goes on behind the scenes in a Post Office, or someone selling tickets on the Internet.

About this Unit

This unit will help you to identify a range of business activities and to find useful ways of grouping them for investigation. It will also help you to recognise the different ways in which businesses can be owned. You will be able to answer such questions as:

You will also learn about differences in business activity in different areas. For example, what differences would you expect to find between businesses in a country area and businesses in a city?

Do businesses change their activities over time? Why? To what extent is this the result of new competition from other businesses?

You should be able to understand how the businesses you investigate for your portfolio fit in to the overall patterns of business activity across the country.

What is the difference between a business run by one person and one with partners?

Is it a good idea to have lots of shareholders in a business?

Why does the government get involved in running some businesses?

2 Who are fish fingers for?

Fancy a fish finger?

Do you fancy fish fingers for tea, or a chargrill burger? We are all used to frozen foods as part of our diet, but how many of us stop to think about the businesses that produce these products?

Birds Eye Wall's is probably the best known of all the frozen food manufacturers in the UK. Owned by the Anglo-Dutch Unilever Group, Birds Eye Wall's has factories at a number of locations in the country, including two in Humberside. Between them, the Hull and Grimsby factories produce a wide range of products for the UK and continental markets. The Hull factory produces fish fingers and other fish recipes such as cod in sauce. It also has the world's largest pea-processing plant. The Grimsby factory makes a whole range of meals including roast dinners, lasagne and curries.

Birds Eye Wall's is committed to good quality products and maintaining a quality service to the customer. As part of its drive for a 'world-class image', Birds Eye Wall's has achieved national and international quality standards such as **ISO 9002**. A good quality product and business image encourages big supermarkets to stock popular and less well-known goods.

Birds Eye Wall's is always prepared to work in partnership with its customers. It aims to do this by providing the best possible service to the customer, by exceeding their expectations and by responding to customer demand with new product ideas. Birds Eye Wall's hopes that this partnership will result in satisfied customers who will choose to buy the products for their quality and because they represent value for money.

IN TRAY

1 What products does Birds Eye Wall's produce?

2 Who are Birds Eye Wall's' customers?

3 Why is it important for Birds Eye Wall's to make products that achieve a national quality standard?

4 Apart from food products, what other goods do you and your family buy? How do you know if these goods are of a high standard?

Consumer goods

Many manufacturing businesses make a profit from the production of **consumer goods**. These businesses can be very large and produce many different products at factories around the UK and abroad. As consumers, we are more likely to know the product name – such as Birds Eye Wall's fish fingers – than the name of the business that owns it – Unilever.

Smaller manufacturers may make consumer goods from just one factory or base, and may sell them in one local area. Dairy products are an example where consumers may know of the dairy but not the farm that produces local milk.

Some businesses make consumer goods that are bought regularly by most consumers. Petrol and bread are examples of products bought nationwide by adults of different ages and with different incomes. Other goods, such as spicy sausages or hiking clothes, may be bought by particular groups in a few areas of the country. Goods such as televisions, computers and cars are bought less often, and businesses may have to compete hard for customers.

Success and profit for all such businesses depend on consumers:

◆ knowing about the products

◆ liking the quality and the price of the products

◆ being able to buy products when and where they like

CHECKPOINT

1 Work with others to make a list of five goods that you and your family buy weekly, monthly and yearly.

2 Use your list of goods to decide:
(a) which goods are available nationwide;
(b) which are made locally and sold only in local shops.

3 Unemployment is rising and consumers are worried about the future. How might this situation affect businesses that made (a) biscuits and cakes, and (b) cars?

KEY TERMS

☞ **Consumer goods** are goods that are manufactured for sale to the general public.

☞ **ISO 9002** is the international standard that recognises a company has achieved a consistently high standard of operation.

3 Train spotting

OBJECTIVES

To learn that some businesses provide services rather than products in order to make a profit.

On the right track?

Anglia Railways is one of the smallest of the train-operating businesses in the UK. Based in Ipswich, it provides both Intercity expresses from Norwich to London and local rural services, which it operates to most towns in Norfolk and Suffolk.

The company has concentrated on providing a high-quality service to its customers, offering:

- a range of tickets to suit all needs
- free seat reservations
- free local bus travel
- an international service to Holland in partnership with Stena Line

- a restaurant/buffet facility on all Intercity services
- a trolley service with light refreshments on all Intercity services
- a Business Club
- a Commuter Club
- a bus link from Colchester to Stansted airport
- facilities for cyclists

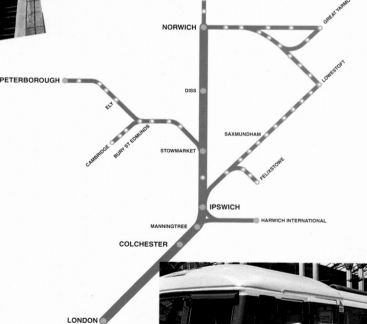

88

Anglia Railways faces competition from another train company and from coach operators. Many consumers could also choose to use their private cars for the journeys. A business priority is thus to ensure maximum satisfaction for its customers. The business was the first rail company to receive a **Charter Mark** award for the quality of its operations.

In addition, Anglia Railways recently upgraded its services by improving the frequency of trains from Norwich to London to every half hour during the day. This has been done by purchasing new three-coach trains. Local services have also been improved by the introduction of through-services to London from towns such as Lowestoft and Bury St Edmunds. The new trains are currently the only ones in the UK that provide full facilities for travellers with disabilities.

IN TRAY

1. What do consumers buy from Anglia Railways?

2. What differences in service might be expected by a local train customer and one travelling on the Intercity to London?

3. What has Anglia Railways done to improve the service offered to the customer?

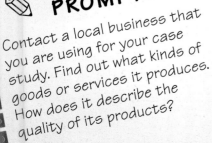

PORTFOLIO PROMPTS

Contact a local business that you are using for your case study. Find out what kinds of goods or services it produces. How does it describe the quality of its products?

Selling services

Many businesses provide services rather than goods for consumers. Travel firms offer international flights, rail journeys and local bus services. Hotels provide rooms and meals, while banks offer savings schemes, safe storage and management of money. In effect, to buy a service is to buy someone else's time and skill.

The personal touch is very important in the **service sector**. Consumers will return to a particular hairdresser or restaurant for all sorts of reasons. It can be difficult to decide when a business has improved its services. Anglia Railways might record how many train services are provided and how many run on time; a consumer might be more concerned with the seat room, the quality of food and the friendliness of staff on the trains.

In the UK, more people work in businesses providing services than in businesses making goods. This can be seen in the local high street. All shops provide a service, because that is where products can be found. But look closely at the products they sell and you'll notice that many of them are consumer services.

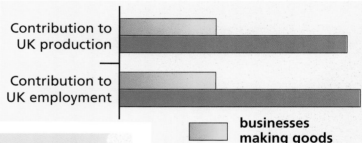

Contribution to UK production

Contribution to UK employment

☐ businesses making goods

☐ businesses providing services

ACTION

1. Working in groups, identify businesses that provide transport services for goods or people.

2. Identify some local businesses that provide services as their main business activity. What could be used to measure the quality of these services?

3. As well as selling consumer goods in their stores, supermarkets are keen to compete in providing a quality service to customers. What is important to you in choosing a supermarket for shopping?

KEY TERMS

⚷ **Service sector** is the name given to the group of businesses whose main activity is to provide consumer services.

⚷ **Charter Mark** is a national award given to businesses that meet a given set of standards.

4 Businesses need machines

OBJECTIVES

To find out about capital goods and be able to identify businesses that make them.

Making robots

ABB is a very large business that makes robots for use in manufacturing of all kinds. It introduced the world's first all-electric robot in 1974, and now offers the latest industrial models.

The robots are capable of performing a number of activities, including welding metal, gluing and sealing components together, looking after other machines, and collecting different items from around a warehouse.

The robots are built to meet the needs of each of ABB's business customers. ABB provides expert help to fit and service the machines, and to train staff. It has customers in America, Europe and the Far East. A major UK customer is Rover Cars, which uses robots to help in handling heavy metal materials, in the assembly process, and in spraying the car bodies.

PORTFOLIO PROMPTS

- Does the business that you are investigating make capital goods?

- What capital goods does it use? Why has it chosen the ones it uses? Have they been updated recently?

IN TRAY

1 What product does ABB make?

2 Who are ABB's customers?

3 ABB's success depends on the success of businesses like Rover Cars. Explain this statement.

Why is machinery important?

Rover Cars has many business rivals, so it has to keep costs down. One way of doing this is to use the latest machinery in the production process. While the

machines are expensive to design and fit to meet Rover's particular needs, they will save costs in the future. Fewer workers will be needed and the robots can work for 24-hour shifts without extra pay.

Robots also help to improve the quality of products because they can work to a high degree of accuracy and do not get tired. In the design workshop, computer-aided design, or **CAD**, means that staff can produce high-quality drawings and simulate a variety of shapes and tests. Computer-controlled production lines allow for the best of assembly-line methods but can tailor each car's assembly and extras to the exact needs of customers.

This does, of course, mean that ABB will be assured of regular business as it supports staff and services machinery in the years ahead.

Capital goods and consumer goods

Manufacturing businesses can be divided into two different groups: those that produce consumer goods, like Birds Eye on p. 86, and those that produce **capital goods**, like ABB. Capital goods are made for other businesses to use in their production processes. As well as being interesting machines, ABB robots are important because they are used by businesses like Rover to make cars.

Capital goods are necessary for efficient production today and in the future. The success of capital goods manufacturers is very closely tied to the success of their own business customers. Firms usually order machinery a long way in advance, so that it takes a while before a slump in business activity hits capital goods. On the other hand, a rise in consumer spending will take a while before it leads to new orders for machinery.

ABB also finds that its business orders are affected by changes in interest rates. It is more difficult for firms to borrow money to buy machines when interest rates are high. If businesses can pay for machinery from their own profits, then interest rates are less important.

IN TRAY

1 What are the costs and benefits that Rover Cars has to consider when installing robots on its assembly lines?

2 Why are ABB's business customers unlikely to be small firms?

ACTION

1 New capital goods are expensive. What would you need to consider if you were a Rover Cars manager who has received a request from your production controller for more machinery?

2 You are a manager of a small hairdressing business. In what situation would you consider buying expensive equipment for colouring and perming hair?

KEY TERMS

○┳┛ **Capital goods** are goods for businesses to use in the manufacture of other products.

○┳┛ **CAD** is computer-aided design – the use of computers to assist in the design process.

5 What's at the core?

Just cows?

If you drink milk, have you ever thought about how a dairy farm operates as a business, and what the influences on the business are?

Manor Farm is a small dairy farm of approximately 228 acres in eastern Suffolk. It rents a further 100 acres of grassland to provide room for its cattle. There are 120 milk-producing cows, which are milked twice a day, producing on average 30 litres of milk. The milk is sold to Milk Marque, a national organisation responsible for setting the price of milk, who sell it on to processors to produce bottled milk, creams and yoghurts. Two years ago the milk was worth 25 pence a litre, but the current price has dropped to around 18 pence a litre. This drop in the price of milk has had a major effect on the profitability of the farm.

Manor Farm, like many others, is unable to increase the production of milk because of a limit set by the **European Union**. This means that the farm must keep its operation under constant review in order to remain profitable. As well as producing milk, Manor Farm grows wheat for sale on the open market and barley and oats, which are kept for animal feed.

Gary Tomkins Manor Farm

> We've got the skills, the expertise and a lot of machinery tied up in milk. We like to think we do this very well, but there's always room for improvement. The trouble is, we're not sure what future prices for milk will be like. We have to think about other activities and keep our hand in with crops like wheat.

IN TRAY

1 What is the main activity undertaken at Manor Farm?

2 What other activities take place on the farm?

3 For what reasons has Manor Farm concentrated on one main activity?

4 If the business outlook was positive, why might Manor Farm prefer to grow a wider range of crops rather than expand its dairy herd?

ACTION

Look again at the activities of Birds Eye on p. 86. Do you think the business has a core activity? What do you consider to be the core activities provided by your school for pupil and parent consumers?

Businesses with a core of activities

Like Manor Farm, many businesses tend to specialise in a particular activity. This central activity is called the core of the business. Businesses don't always plan to have a **core activity** but may find it to be a good idea. There are a number of reasons for this:

◆ The business has access to materials, or skilled labour.

◆ Specialists can get a good reputation for a quality product or service.

◆ The business is able to train its staff to do a certain job.

◆ Specialists can buy machinery to become more efficient, and make better profits.

There are risks in sticking to one activity or to a limited range of activities.

◆ Consumer tastes may change so the product is no longer wanted.

◆ It is hard to change to other activities when money has been spent on specialist equipment.

◆ If costs of materials go up, the specialist activity may not be so profitable.

How does a core activity develop?

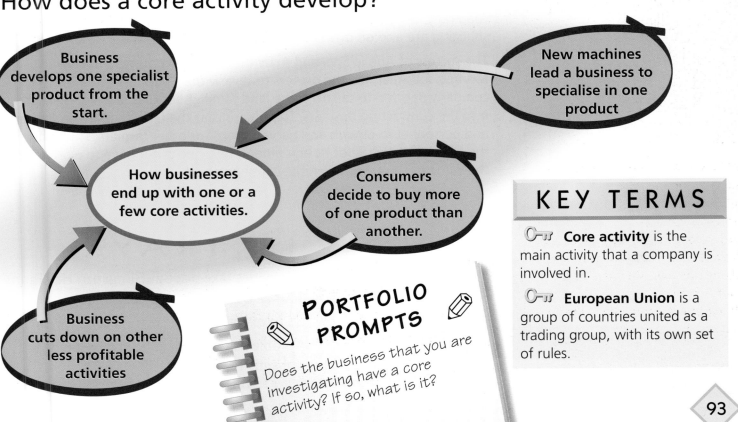

Business develops one specialist product from the start.

New machines lead a business to specialise in one product

How businesses end up with one or a few core activities.

Consumers decide to buy more of one product than another.

Business cuts down on other less profitable activities

KEY TERMS

⊶ **Core activity** is the main activity that a company is involved in.

⊶ **European Union** is a group of countries united as a trading group, with its own set of rules.

PORTFOLIO PROMPTS

Does the business that you are investigating have a core activity? If so, what is it?

6 A farm with a difference

A sporting chance

Mud Bugs, paintball, clay pigeon shooting and team-building activities – not the sorts of things you'd normally associate with a farm.

Hungarian Hall Farm is a farm with a difference. Bought 25 years ago by the Boardley family as a 400-acre arable farm, its only activity was growing and harvesting cereal crops. However, changes in farming subsidies led to a drop in earnings and the family had to consider other possible areas for generating income.

The first venture was the introduction of paintball in 1988, and Anglia Sporting Activities was born. The business specialises in a range of exciting activities, including entertainment for business staff and team-building courses. One area of the farm has been set aside for paintball adventure games. An outdoor racing circuit built to national guidelines provides off-road rally karting at various levels. Lasersport and simulated clay pigeon shooting are also on offer at the complex.

The success of Anglia Sporting Activities, and the continued decline in farming subsidies, led the owners to review their business activities. The company decided to sell off some land to neighbouring farms and enter into the contracting business. This means that the farm supplies equipment and personnel to plough and harvest crops for other farmers. This allows the farm to make use of its equipment, but it does not have to worry about the value of the crops when they are harvested.

IN TRAY

1 What activities take place at Hungarian Hall Farm?

2 What other non-farming activities might the owners have considered?

3 What problems could there be in developing a range of activities?

Core and peripheral activities

Many businesses have core and **peripheral activities**. Sometimes this is as a result of take-overs or acquisitions by other businesses. As the new organisation expands, the range of activities undertaken by the business is also likely to grow. In other cases it is due to constraints on the business and a need to survive by expanding into new areas. Anglia Sporting Activities is a good example of this.

For a business to be successful, it must constantly reappraise its core and diverse activities to ensure that they remain profitable.

Supermarkets are another example of businesses that have a range of activities. Tesco, for example, has moved from its core business of food sales to clothing and now into banking and computing services.

Granada is a business with a range of activities in entertainment and leisure services. Its activities include running a regional television network, managing Posthouse Hotels and Little Chef fast-food restaurants, and renting televisions. Granada attracts a wide range of customers to buy a variety of services. In a fast-changing world, it is likely that some of its business activities will be successful.

Granada

Hospitality

TV Rental

Media

ACTION

Find out which of the following businesses are involved in a range of activities: Debenham's, Virgin Radio, Carphone Warehouse, McDonald's, Gap, Sony. Why do you think they have kept to a core or broadened their range of activities?

CHECKPOINT

1 What products are sold by both supermarkets and petrol stations?

2 What do you think are the core activities and the diverse activities of these two kinds of business?

3 Write a short paragraph to explain the connections between Granada's various business activities.

PORTFOLIO PROMPTS

Find out if the business that you are investigating has core and peripheral activities.

KEY TERM

🔑 **Peripheral activities** are additional activities that are different to the main activity of a business.

7 Local business – it's different

What's there?

Framlingham is a small market town in a **rural** part of Suffolk. The main business in the area is farming, with a range of different farms from mixed and arable farms to dairy and pig farms. Several other businesses in Framlingham support the activities of the farming industry. These include a farm trailer manufacturer, a supplier of farm machinery, a seed merchant and a pet food processor. A farmers' group is involved in the purchase of seed, specialist countryside training and farming insurance. There is also a vet's practice.

The town has a range of shops, which include a supermarket, clothes shops, grocery shops, a butcher's, a baker's, banks and financial services, estate agents, pubs and a hotel. At the edge of town there is a small industrial estate, with a company that makes streamlined sleeper cabs for lorries, and a number of hi-tech design and computer companies.

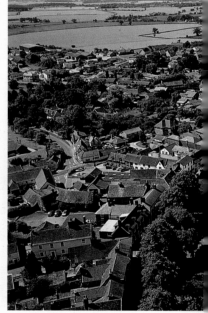

IN TRAY

1. What is the main kind of business activity in Framlingham?

2. Draw a chart to show the links between the business activities in Framlingham. Use a colour code to show which activities involve consumer goods, capital goods and services.

ACTION

1 Use a guide like the *Yellow Pages* to find a sample of local businesses. Look for businesses that may have special links to others in the area.

2 Talk to an adult who remembers the local businesses from 20 years ago. What changes have taken place? What businesses still survive?

3 If you represented your local area at a national conference, what could you say about your area that might attract a new business.

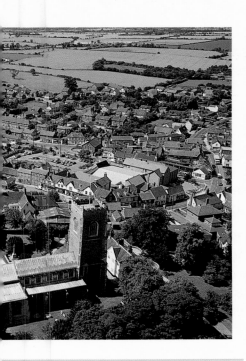

Local businesses

Some businesses can be found in every local area. A grocery shop, a bank, a pub and a Post Office are among a range of businesses needed by every community. But if you looked for a job in your area or carried out a survey, you would notice how many **local businesses** have their own special features.

Country towns like Framlingham grow up with many people earning a living from farming. Farmers need suppliers, auctions, repair services and others to keep their businesses running smoothly.

The countryside may attract visitors, so a small town may have a surprising number of hotels and other services. An area of land may be cleared and a small industrial estate built. The businesses moving in may bring completely new kinds of jobs and products to the community. The local council may even promote the area to businesses elsewhere, and it can be strange to see your local area being advertised like other 'products'.

Some local communities have one large business that provides most of the local jobs. A large airport, a mail-order company or a leisure theme park may attract other linked businesses to the area. The benefits are obvious, but a local community can be devastated if a major employer moves away.

3 What might happen to a supplier of farm machinery, a vet and a local clothes shop if Framlingham farmers were making a loss from their businesses?

PORTFOLIO PROMPTS

Find out if the businesses you are studying have any special links, past or present, to your local community or to other local businesses.

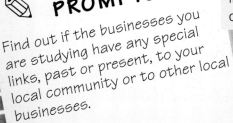

KEY TERMS

○━ **Rural area** is an area of the country that is mainly agricultural.

○━ **Local business** is a business to be found in the immediate area of your town or district.

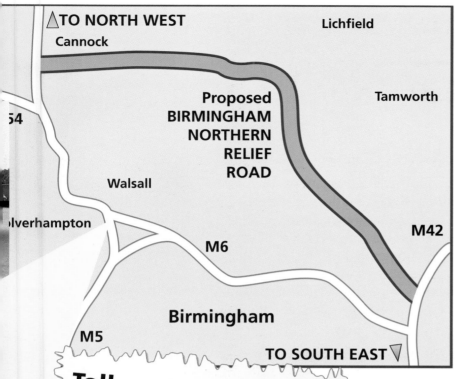

TO NORTH WEST

Cannock

Lichfield

Proposed
BIRMINGHAM
NORTHERN
RELIEF
ROAD

Tamworth

54

Walsall

lverhampton

M6

M42

Birmingham

M5

TO SOUTH EAST

Time is money

A location with easy access to a motorway may save hours of travel time. Some countries have encouraged businesses to send goods by rail. This is cheap and effective once the goods are at the freight terminal. In the UK, however, many businesses have invested in lorries and would be reluctant to change. They would like to see more money spent on new roads, which isn't always popular. Some countries are concerned about the environmental damage caused by excessive use of roads, and have introduced extra taxes on fuel, tolls on motorways and higher taxes for big freight vehicles.

Toll motorway gets green light

The High Court has cleared the way for work to continue on the Birmingham Northern Relief Road (BNRR). The 27-mile Relief Road has been planned to take traffic off the M6. The M6 motorway just north of Birmingham is one of the busiest stretches of road in Europe.

Protesters tried to stop the development because it runs through the greenbelt countryside around the city. The £700 million motorway will be the first in the UK to be built and managed by a private business, Midland Expressway. Midland Expressway says the road is needed by business to speed up transportation between Scotland, the north and southern England.

Source: BBC Online News, 23 March 1999

IN TRAY

1 Why are campaigners trying to stop the BNRR being built?

2 Why do the builders of the BNRR say that it is needed?

3 Why do you think motorways are important for many businesses?

ACTION

Draw a map showing the major transport links in the area where you live (motorways and main roads, main rail links, and any airports or ports). How easy would it be for your local businesses to reach customers in Europe? Where are the greatest delays likely for road freight?

PORTFOLIO PROMPTS

Find out how important transport links are to the business you are investigating. Use the map you produced for your area and link it to the business.

KEY TERMS

Distribution is the delivery of goods from factory to sales outlet.

Logistics is the section of a business dealing with transport and distribution.

Road haulage firms are businesses that specialise in delivering goods by road.

13 Make it local

The corner shop

Most of us have a newsagent's shop close to where we live, usually within walking distance. A typical newsagent's shop sells newspapers, magazines, stationery, sweets and some other types of food, and it may also rent out videos and deliver newspapers to people's homes. It could be located in a residential area where there are no other shops or newsagents nearby, or on the corner of two busy main roads. It may have a customer car park, or it could be near a bus stop on the main road. It may be close to a large housing estate.

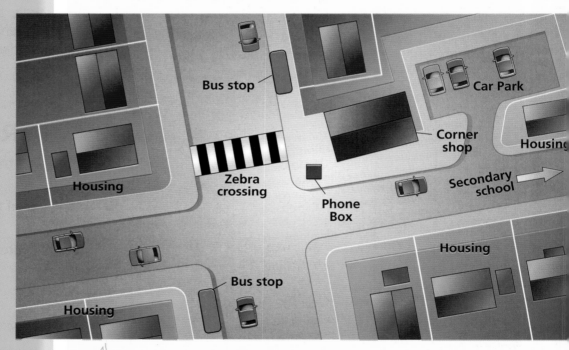

Bus stop · Car Park · Corner shop · Housing · Housing · Zebra crossing · Phone Box · Secondary school · Housing · Bus stop · Housing

IN TRAY

1 Explain why each of the following features might be important for the shop:
   (a) a main road; (b) a car park;
   (c) a bus stop; (d) a housing estate.

2 What do you think would happen if another newsagent's shop opened nearby?

3 How do you think the shop would be affected if a fish and chip shop opened nearby?

4 What type of people do you think are likely to b the shop's main customers?

Customers

Without customers, a business cannot survive. The types of customers a business has depends on the products or services it makes or sells. The corner shop's customers live nearby and pop in to buy things when it is convenient. They do not travel far or spend very much.

Some small shops locate on busy roads and attract a lot of passing trade. Some sell specialist goods and customers travel a long way to buy their products.

Some businesses can travel easily to meet customers. Computer consultants and designers can often use customer **premises** for most of their day-to-day contact. This keeps costs down.

Cost of location

Every location has a cost. A business must buy or rent its premises and pay **business rates** to the local council. It is more expensive to buy land in a city or town than in a remote rural area, and more expensive to **rent** a shop in a city centre than in a **suburb**. The cost of renting premises in a **residential area** is generally less than in a business centre.

To afford a site in the city centre, a shop would need to have a lot of customers who spend a lot of money. This would give it a large enough turnover to be able to afford the rent. For this reason, it is mainly high-street chain stores such as Marks & Spencer and Bhs that are found in town centres.

Similarly, a small business would find it hard to afford the rent in a new industrial estate, but might afford older premises tucked away in a side street.

ACTION

Investigate the location of a local newsagent's shop. Draw a map to show the location. On your map show any important features such as other shops, roads, car parks, bus stops and housing. Describe the main advantages and disadvantages of the shop's location.

CHECKPOINT

1 Why do you think it is more expensive to rent premises in a city centre than in a remote rural area?

2 Why do you think people do not want to travel a long way to buy the things the corner shop sells?

3 A hairdresser moves from a corner shop on a housing estate to a busy high-street site. Rent and rates go up. How could the business cover the extra cost?

KEY TERMS

🔑 **Business rates** are a kind of tax paid by businesses to the local council.

🔑 **Rent** is paid by a business for the use of the premises.

🔑 A **suburb** is part of a town or city away from the centre.

🔑 **Premises** are the buildings that a business uses.

🔑 **Residential area** is an area that mostly contains housing.

PORTFOLIO PROMPTS

- For the business you are investigating, find out who are the main customers and where they are located. Have there been any changes in the types of customer the business has?

- Try to find out about the cost of renting or buying the premises.

14 A helping hand

OBJECTIVES

To find out how financial help from the government influences location.

Why Wales?

If you owned your own business, would you consider locating in Wales? There are many businesses that have made the decision to do just that. In fact, over 450 foreign companies have sites in Wales, including such well-known businesses as Sony, Aiwa, Ford and Toyota.

One organisation that has played an important role in bringing industry into Wales is the Welsh Development Agency (WDA). The WDA is a government body that aims to attract companies to Wales and provides advice and help to businesses that are setting up. The WDA can:

◆ find suitable sites for factories and offices

◆ help recruit new staff

◆ give advice about grants from the government.

There are many good reasons for businesses to locate in Wales. One important reason is that some businesses are able to receive grants from the government.

ACTION

Find out which areas of the UK are Assisted Areas. Draw your own map to show both the Development and Intermediate Areas. Write a brief explanation of why these areas have been chosen for assistance.

IN TRAY

1 Why do you think it is important to attract foreign companies to Wales?

2 Why do you think it is important to help businesses after they have decided to set up?

How do businesses receive government grants?

Industry in the UK has changed a great deal over the past few decades. Many of the older manufacturing industries have virtually disappeared. This has resulted in a lot of unemployment in some areas.

The government has tried to encourage new industries to set up in these areas. In particular, the government wants to encourage manufacturing businesses to develop, especially those that will create jobs or produce goods for export. To do this it has named some areas as **Assisted Areas**, and businesses that want to set up in these areas can apply for grants to help them.

There are two types of Assisted Areas: **Development Areas**, with very high unemployment rates, and **Intermediate Areas**. Usually, businesses that move into Development Areas can receive larger grants.

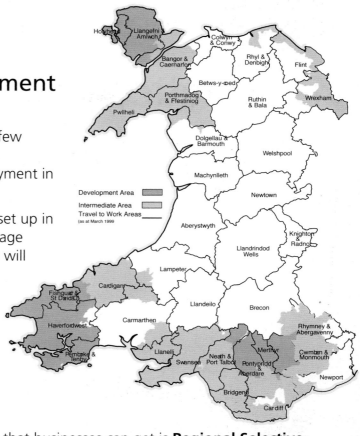

The main grant that businesses can get is **Regional Selective Assistance** to help with the cost of buildings, land, plant and machinery. Altogether there are more than 250 different kinds of financial assistance that businesses can receive. Businesses have to apply for grants before they begin their investment, and it can be worth up to 15 per cent of certain costs.

The amount of grant that is awarded to a business will depend on the area in which it is to be located, the number of jobs safeguarded or created, the needs of the investor and the overall impact on the economy.

CHECKPOINT

1 Why is there high unemployment in some areas?

2 Which types of business does the government want to set up in these areas?

3 Why do you think Development Areas are worth larger grants than Intermediate Areas?

4 What types of grants can businesses receive and what can they be used for?

KEY TERMS

⚿ **Assisted Area** is an overall name for areas where businesses are assisted in setting up.

⚿ **Development Areas** are areas with a very high unemployment rate.

⚿ **Intermediate Areas** are areas with above-average unemployment levels.

⚿ **Regional Selective Assistance** is a type of grant that businesses can receive from the government.

PORTFOLIO PROMPTS

Find out if the business you are investigating is located in an Assisted Area. If it is, find out if it received any grants from the government.

15 Location free

On the phone

You have probably seen the red telephone that Direct Line uses as its logo and heard the musical jingle that announces its arrival. Direct Line is the UK's largest private motor insurance company.

When the company was launched in 1985, it was the first insurance company to use the telephone as its primary sales tool. The idea was that by dealing with the public directly, it could cut out the middle step and thereby offer people cheaper motor insurance. Direct Line has centres in six major UK cities, but customers are able to call them from anywhere in the country.

A computerised telephone system is able to re-route hundreds of calls per second around Direct Line's network spanning the six cities so that customers are not kept waiting. A customer may ring the Bristol number but actually speak to someone in Glasgow. The company handles more than 15 million calls each year.

This method of selling a service using the telephone proved so successful that Direct Line has extended its services to cover home insurance, breakdown insurance, mortgages, personal loans and others.

On-line shopping

Hawkshead is an organisation that sells outdoor clothing. After starting the business with one shop in the village of Hawkshead in Cumbria, it now has several shops in other areas of the country.

ACTION

Find out what types of items or services you are able to buy on the Internet.

IN TRAY

1 In how many different ways can a customer buy goods from Hawkshead?

2 Is it true to say that Hawkshead could not locate anywhere?

In the future

Better motorway systems and improved communications through mobile phones, Ceefax and the like mean that many businesses worry less about location.

The use of the telephone has changed the way that many businesses operate. **On-line shopping** also makes use of the telephone, linked to a computer with a modem. Organisations do not need to have shops where customers can view the items on sale. Customers from all over the country, or even the world, can have access to the same products or services.

An on-line business order has to be translated into actual products. A warehouse and transport service will be necessary at some stage. Electronic orders rely on the customer using a bank account or credit card. This means that the system has to be able to prevent fraud. It also means that businesses will not have any young customers. (You have to be an adult with a good bank account to use a credit card.)

Shopping on the Internet is a growing area and is likely to have a big influence on the way we shop in the future.

IN TRAY

1 Why do you think Direct Line's method of selling insurance over the telephone has been so successful?

2 Why does Direct Line not need to locate its centres close to where all of its customers live?

3 Why do you think Direct Line's methods of selling over the telephone might not have been so successful ten years earlier?

In addition, Hawkshead uses other ways of gaining more customers: it offers a **mail-order shopping** service, telephone orders and on-line shopping through the Internet. Customers pay using their credit or debit card.

3 Which sales method do you think will be most widely used in ten years time?

CHECKPOINT

1 What are the advantages for businesses of selling on the Internet or by telephone?

2 What are the advantages for customers of shopping on the Internet?

3 What is likely to be the problem for someone under 18 trying to buy some clothes on the Internet?

KEY TERMS

○━┓ **Mail-order shopping** is using a catalogue to buy and sell goods through the post.

○━┓ **On-line shopping** is buying goods or services through the Internet.

PORTFOLIO PROMPTS

Find out if the business you are investigating has a website. If so, what is it used for?

16 Where's the competition?

OBJECTIVES
To find out about how competition affects the location of businesses.

What a choice

Like most young people, you probably like shopping for clothes. When you go shopping you're likely to go to a town or city shopping centre where there are lots of different clothes shops. Most people like to have a choice of shops so that they can find exactly what they want at the best price.

The Fort Shopping Park in Birmingham is a shopping centre that has several clothes shops, such as Next, Principles, Suit Direct, Oasis, Top Shop, Burtons and River Island. The shopping centre is very popular because there's a good range of shops and lots of choice. When you are out shopping, you might also go somewhere for something to eat or drink. The Fort Shopping Park has a choice of eating places for shoppers, including Burger King, Druckers, Fat Jackets and Fatty Arbuckles.

Competition – good or bad?

Competition occurs when businesses are trying to sell their goods or services to the same customers.

The Fort Shopping Park is attractive to customers because it offers plenty of choice. The businesses there benefit from the competition provided by other similar businesses. In this example, competition can be an advantage. Many shops locate in large shopping centres because of the number of customers available to them.

For some businesses, competition can be a bad thing. For example, a chip shop that is located in a small shopping area where there are no other chip shops would suffer if another one opened nearby. Both shops would be competing for the same small number of customers.

All around the world

Many businesses operate on a global scale, so competition can be worldwide. This is particularly true for large manufacturing organisations. For example, all the major car manufacturers such as

CHECKPOINT

1 Why do high street banks often choose sites alongside each other?

2 Why is nearby competition likely to be a problem for a small fish and chip shop?

3 Why do some companies open factories in developing countries?

4 Explain how a company operating only in the UK can be affected by **foreign competition**.

IN TRAY

1   Why do you think people are attracted to the Fort Shopping Park?

2   Why is it important to have restaurants in a shopping centre?

3   Why do you think it is important for people to have a choice when they are shopping?

4   Do you think there are any disadvantages for shops in being located close together?

Ford, Vauxhall, Honda, Toyota, Peugeot and Rover are in competition with each other all over the world.

Because of competition, businesses have to keep their prices as low as possible. To do this they have to keep their costs low. Many businesses are able to reduce their production costs by locating their factories in developing countries where labour costs are much lower. Even businesses that operate only in the UK may be in competition with businesses from abroad. A business manufacturing items and selling them in the UK can be affected by companies from abroad that are making similar items and also selling them in the UK.

ACTION

Investigate a small shopping area close to where you live. Draw a map of the centre and make lists of the shops you think are in competition with each other. Choose one of the shops and write a short report explaining why the owner chose the site.

PORTFOLIO PROMPTS

- For the business you are investigating, find out who are its main competitors, what they do and where they are located.

- What effect is this competition having on the business?

KEY TERMS

🔑 **Competition** is when businesses are selling similar goods or services to the same group of customers.

🔑 **Foreign competition** is competition with businesses in other countries.

119

16a Why businesses relocate

Boro's plans on the table

Detailed plans have been unveiled for the new Nuneaton Borough soccer ground. Boro are set to kick off in a big way with an ambitious plan to build a brand new £4.2 million stadium.

Following years of speculation about the future of the Manor Park headquarters, the Nationwide Conference league club is on the verge of a new future. A site has already been earmarked at the former quarry and waste tip bordering Bermuda Road, and detailed plans for a stadium, practice pitch, car parking and landscaping have been drawn up.

Club Chairman Phil Clayton said: 'The site is not too far away from our present ground and has the advantage of good access. Manor Park has been the home of football in Nuneaton for more than 60 years, so it will be a wrench to leave.'

The ground will be built in phases with an initial capacity of 6,500, including 1,500 seated to meet Football League standards. This could be increased later to almost 10,000, with everyone seated. There would be 100 places designed for supporters with disabilities and hospitality boxes providing high-class places for 129 people.

There are also plans for a banqueting room, a fitness centre, conference centre, a new grass pitch for use by local schools, and a football academy for training boys and girls.

ACTION

Find out if there are any businesses in your area that have changed location. Choose one business and compare the old and new locations, thinking of the advantages and disadvantages of each.

IN TRAY

1 Why does Nuneaton Borough want to move to a new ground?

2 Why is the new site likely to be a suitable location for the club?

3 Who will benefit from the move to a new ground?

4 Why might some supporters not be happy about the move?

Why relocate?

The newspaper article shows that Nuneaton Borough Football Club is keen to join the growing list of football clubs at all levels who are moving to new grounds.

Many football grounds were built in the late 1990s. The law now requires higher standards of safety at a public stadium, and clubs have had to make the decision to upgrade their current ground, or sell it and build a more up-to-date stadium. It is usually the case that if it doesn't have modern facilities, the club misses out on promotion.

Clubs need to find new ways of generating more revenue. New facilities such as a restaurant or conference centre will allow this to happen. Many old sites are in areas that are more suitable for housing than for sports arenas. Profits can often be made by selling the ground for housing and buying cheaper out-of-city land for a new stadium.

The majority of football fans travel to matches by car and need somewhere to park. Football fans in the 2000s expect to be seated for matches, and expect places to eat or drink and decent toilets.

A similar situation occurs with other types of businesses. Some shops find that the premises they occupy are no longer suitable and they move to larger ones when they become available. The costs of **relocation** can be offset against the higher number of customers spending more money in the new shop.

A manufacturing business may move because the reasons for the existing site have become less important. New customers in Europe could lure a business away from the north of England towards the south with the thought of lower transport costs.

New technology may also require a large-scale reorganisation of the factory. It could be cheaper to move to a new purpose-built site than to try to adapt the old one.

CHECKPOINT

1 How have football supporters' expectations changed?

2 How does moving to a new ground allow clubs to generate more revenue?

3 How are clubs able to afford to build the new grounds?

4 Why might a business selling its own in-car music systems wish to move site from small premises in a side road to a new retail park on the edge of town?

KEY TERMS

⚷ **Relocation** means to move to another site.

⚷ **Retail park** is a modern term to describe a purpose-built set of buildings that can be used for shopping and business.

PORTFOLIO PROMPTS

Find out if the business you are investigating has changed location in the past, or might be considering relocating. What are the reasons for the change or possible change?

16b How businesses develop

Headline news

M40 brings about Banbury expansion

Supermarkets to open 24 hours a day

Another out-of-town superstore to open

Wage levels in south continue to rise

IN TRAY

1 The M40 passes just east of Banbury. Why do you think this has brought about a growth of industry in the town?

2 Why do you think some shops feel it is necessary to open long hours?

3 Why do you think more and more stores are opening on the outskirts of UK towns and cities?

4 What effect is the level of wages likely to have on a business considering locating in the south of England?

A changing world

The world of business is never still. The four headlines provide examples of the kinds of change taking place. No organisation operates in complete isolation, so external factors can influence location as well as other decisions.

◆ The motorway influence

Banbury is just one example of how the importance of a town's location can change with the building of a motorway. When the M40 opened in 1991, it improved access between the south-east and the West Midlands. Industry has been attracted to the town because of this improved access. This can have a knock-on-effect. More people with more money to spend means more business for shops and leisure facilities. The motorways bring their own linked developments, too: services, travel hotels and associated businesses.

◆ Out-of-town shopping

One growing trend has been the development of out-of-town shopping. There is hardly a town without a large DIY superstore or supermarket somewhere on the outskirts. People want to travel by car and town centres are no place for drivers, with their lack of parking and congested streets. More than 5,000 stores are now located on the edge of town, with numbers ever increasing. However, businesses have to get planning permission from local councils, which may not be easy if there is countryside to preserve around a town.

◆ Take-overs

Take-overs of one business by another occur regularly. This allows a business to expand into a new area without having to build new premises. A recent and very sizeable example is the take-over of Asda by the American giant company, Wal-Mart.

◆ The Internet

Shopping and business trading on the Internet is described on p. 116. It is growing rapidly and is changing many business habits.

◆ Overseas development

Countries often place restrictions on the number of imports coming into a country. Foreign businesses can overcome such barriers by building a factory in that country. This brings jobs for the home country and greater access to markets for the foreign business.

◆ 24-hour shopping

Businesses are always looking for new ways of attracting customers. One way is to increase business hours, and many supermarkets are now open almost the whole week.

ACTION

Discuss with others how the following business activities have changed over the last ten years. Think carefully about location, external influences and broad business trends.

(a) cinemas
(b) takeaway food outlets
(c) phone services

CHECKPOINT

1 Who benefits and who loses from out-of-town developments?

2 Use an example to explain how taking over a business could give another firm access to a new market.

3 How do you think businesses are likely to respond to the growth in Internet trading?

PORTFOLIO PROMPTS

- How have external influences affected the business you are investigating?

- How has the business responded?

17 Going it alone

Oiling the wheels

John Boate is a car mechanic. He learnt his trade through working for a large car sales company. Twenty years ago, he started his own business. He rented small premises and began mending and servicing cars for friends and others who had heard about him. It was tough in the beginning, as he had to work long hours and do everything himself. He hoped that people whose cars he mended would tell their friends that he did a good job at a fair price.

His business grew steadily, and after six years he was able to employ a mechanic to work with him. His dad helped to keep his records up to date and to check on the cost of running the business.

As time went on, John gained a good reputation. He was able to advertise in the local paper and had signs made to put up outside his yard. His customers now began to include larger businesses with fleets of vehicles that needed regular maintenance. He was now able to employ two mechanics to work with him, as well as a person to work in the office and take care of all the neglected paperwork.

John has to keep a careful eye on his finances. His prices have to be competitive because there are many car repair businesses in the area, but he needs to make enough money to pay the wages of the staff he employs. He needs to buy parts and tools and to pay for electricity, heating and lighting. He also needs to make sure there is enough to pay himself a good salary.

IN TRA

1 What did John do to get his business started successfully

2 What kind of marketing activity was he able to do as the business grew?

Run it yourself

Plumbers, shopkeepers, hairdressers and car maintenance companies are often run by **sole traders**. The owners learn a skill by working for someone else. When they are competent, they start up a business of their own.

There are advantages to being a sole trader. Keeping accounts is less complicated and there is

I didn't have to borrow any money.

I'm happy to stay as I am, me and my business.

Keeping accounts is complicated.

3 What extra responsibilities did he have when he employed staff?

4 Why does he have to keep his prices competitive?

no need to employ an expensive accountant, and there is no need to register the company. However it can be difficult to obtain finance from the bank. The bank likes to see that a business has a good record before it will lend money.

Moving ahead

Two years ago, John moved to bigger premises. He was uncertain about the move at first because the rent would be much higher than he was used to. The premises were on a main road and had petrol pumps and a forecourt. He believed he would attract a lot more business by being more accessible and by selling petrol. John is very glad he made the decision, as he has increased the number of customers and doubled his turnover. He now employs a third mechanic and can work normal hours and take time off.

John's responsibilities have changed since he started his business. In the beginning, he was responsible for his own survival. He had to work until the jobs were finished, and couldn't turn work away or ask people to wait. He would work long into the night writing out invoices and working out how much money he was making. He worried about whether he could pay all his costs. Now he has to look after his staff and make sure they do a good job, as well as motivate them to work hard and do their best. He needs to talk to his larger customers to negotiate discounted rates for the work he does for them. He is keen to keep them, but he is aware that many other companies want the same business, so he has to make sure his prices are competitive.

IN TRAY

1 What were the risks for John of moving into his new premises?

2 What responsibilities does John have towards his mechanics?

3 List some of John's costs that could go up over the next few years. How could he pay for these additional costs?

PORTFOLIO PROMPTS

- Draw up a chart that states the advantages and disadvantages of being a sole trader.

- Write an account of your interview with a sole trader. How has the business changed over recent years?

ACTION

Find a local garage or a similar business run by a sole trader. Interview the owner to find out how he or she started in business and his or her thoughts for the future.

KEY TERMS

 Sole traders are people who run their own business; they may work on their own or employ other staff.

125

Public sector organisations

The government used to run a range of businesses that were of national importance, but many of them have been sold and are now run as plcs. Royal Mail is one of the last in government hands. It sells products and aims to cover its costs. A key purpose, however, is to provide a quality service rather than to make a profit. Sometimes the two go together, although in other situations the search for reduced costs can lead to a lower-quality service.

Public and private businesses have some common objectives, for example:

◆ to be better than any competitors

◆ to find new markets

◆ to design new products

◆ to keep up with new technology

The chairman and the board of directors have the same responsibilities as any business. However, the government sets some of the rules for their business. Royal Mail cannot, for example, borrow money from banks to finance investment, which is one of the reasons why some people say it should move to the **private sector**.

Many of the services that the government provides are expected to work like a business. They have to control the money they receive, and often they sell other services as well. Even the army and the police sell some services. Local councils run leisure centres, which have to cover their costs or face being closed down.

Competition for business?

In recent years, the government has **privatised** many public sector businesses. Shares in British Telecom and British Gas were sold to the public and the businesses became public limited companies. Other private businesses were allowed to compete in areas once reserved for the **public sector**. Some people argue that businesses work better when their main aim is to make profit for shareholders and when they have to compete for business.

Some services are supervised by the government or local councils but are run by private firms. Local leisure centres and school meals are examples. Competition has been introduced by making firms bid against each other to win a contract for a set period of time.

CHECKPOINT

1 How do public sector organisations differ from private sector businesses?

2 Explain the argument for and against privatisation of the Post Office.

ACTION

Compare the business you are studying with a public sector organisation such as your school. In what ways are they similar or different in their objectives and organisation?

KEY TERMS

○┓ **Public sector** refers to council or government-run organisations, whose main aim is to provide service to the whole community.

○┓ **Private sector** refers to businesses owned by individuals and shareholders; a key objective is profit.

○┓ **Privatisation** is the sale of public sector organisations to private shareholders.

23a Business risks and responsibilitie

Managing the risks

John Boate (pp. 124–5) started up his car mechanics business as a sole trader. He didn't want the expense of setting up a limited company and he didn't want to have to keep complicated accounts. His is only a very small business, and he feels confident he can keep track of it. He has sole responsibility for the business as owner, and if the business went bust, he could lose everything he owns.

Mike and Glenda Davidge (pp. 126–7) are in a similar position, though they have a formal agreement as partners about their respective roles in the business.

Franchisees in Appletree Cottage and Candy Cottage (pp. 134–5) are sole traders. They are liable for their business debts, but are sheltered from some of the risks by the experience and support of their franchisers. For example, they have not had to lay out large sums of money to buy premises or stock.

As chairman of Easyjet, Stelios Haji-Ioannou (pp. 128–9) shares the responsibility for managing a fast-growing company with other directors, as does the board of directors at Beatties. Both Easyjet and Beatties are legally registered companies with shareholders who own them. The shareholders have limited liability. If the business went bust, they would lose only their shareholdings, not the rest of their possessions.

The West Midlands Co-operative Society (pp. 132–3) is also a limited company with shareholders who have limited liability. Because the aims of co-operatives are to help members, most of the directors and shareholders have a strong commitment and responsibility to their business.

Wish.
Yo

The Very Best In Greeting
Franchises

From
Appletree Co

CHECKPOINT

1 What is the difference between the liability of a sole trader and of shareholders in a private limited company?

2 Who has responsibility for the key decisions in a partnership and in a public limited company?

3 Explain how a franchise can combine the advantages of a large business and those of a smaller, sole trader.

To be or not to be?

Making a decision to go into business is a very big step to take. Many businesses fail in their first year. It is very risky and requires serious planning, a sound product or service, excellent marketing and a lot of luck.

It is very likely that anyone starting a business will either borrow money or will use savings of their own. Either way, losing that money can have devastating consequences.

The easiest way to start a small business is to become a sole trader. There is no legal requirement to register that you are starting a business, nor is there a need for complicated form-filling or end-of-year accounts. But if the business fails, the owner has **unlimited liability** and could be made to sell personal possessions such as their house or car to pay for the business's debts.

It is more difficult to set up a limited company, but owners have some protection if anything goes wrong and their business fails. They have limited liability. Limited liability means that, provided they have managed the business properly, they will not be responsible for all the debts the business has generated. They will not be expected to sell their personal possessions to pay for the debts. Having limited liability is a privilege and it is very important that directors act in a responsible manner and run the business legally and properly.

The decision about ownership has a lot to do with the size and structure of a business. A very small business is unlikely to need a legal structure to ensure its success. Business owners who need to buy expensive equipment or invest in property of high value may well choose to create a limited company and reduce their liability if anything were to go wrong.

PORTFOLIO PROMPTS

- Contrast two businesses you have investigated and describe clearly each business's type of ownership.
- Explain why the type of ownership suits that business.

KEY TERM

⚬━╗ **Unlimited liability** is where owners are personally responsible for the debts of the business.

24 Who are the stakeholders?

OBJECTIVES

To be able to identify different stakeholders and their interests in a business.

Flying high

Airtours is a tour-operating business which operates from 17 countries on three continents. It has over 20,000 employees and carries over 10 million passengers a year.

Customers are important to the business because they pay for a service. If they enjoy their holiday, they will use Airtours again.

Managers and employees working for Airtours expect to be rewarded for the work they do. Staff costs during the year for wages and salaries were over £26 million. Airtours employees and the company both make contributions towards a staff pension scheme.

CHECKPOINT

1 A business wants to expand its site because there is a big demand for its product. Who would have an interest in the decision to go ahead with the expanded site?

2 Why might the take-over of one company by another be welcomed by some stakeholders and not others?

IN TRAY

1 What groups of people are interested in Airtours being successful? Why?

2 How would each group be affected if Airtours sold fewer holidays?

3 Which groups of people might be described as stakeholders of McDonald's?

Which stakeholders?

Stakeholders are all those individuals and groups of people who have an interest in the way a business works. Sometimes their interests are the same, and sometimes there are conflicts between the groups.

Other businesses such as hotels and aircraft suppliers deal with Airtours. These businesses depend on Airtours to settle their bills in order to carry on trading.

In 1998 there were 5,565 Airtours shareholders, who received a dividend of £7.50 per share.

Airtours Group has a bank loan of £51 million. This makes the bank one of Airtours' creditors.

A business cannot exist in isolation from the local community. Airtours Group helps the community in the UK and abroad, and makes considerable donations to various national and international charities.

Airtours has to take account of the 17 different governments in whose airspace it travels. The business has to comply with the rules and regulations within each country.

Local community. A business cannot exist in isolation from the community surrounding it. Business employees spend money in local shops. Local councils decide on planning rules and inspect health and safety conditions. Businesses can help a community with projects to improve the environment, or give money to support local charities and schools.

Pressure groups such as a trade union or the environmental group Greenpeace try to influence business to make decisions to suit their members. They may organise protests locally, nationally and internationally.

Owners, shareholders and **creditors** directly invest money in the business. Shareholders risk their money buying a share and expect to collect a dividend each year. Owners put in their own money and hope to make a profit. Creditors such as banks lend money to the business in return for payment.

Business

Suppliers rely on a fair and regular trading relationship. They need to receive payments for materials in good time.

Managers and employees spend time working for the company and depend on the business to get paid. They have a right to work in fair and safe conditions. Employees' attitudes and skills influence the success of the business.

Customers buy the products. They rely on the product doing the job it was bought for and being safe.

Government. The government helps to regulate business using the laws of the land. Government economic policy may help or hinder businesses. Governments also need the support of business.

4 In what ways do you think stakeholders of McDonald's might have similar or different interests in the business?

KEY TERMS

Creditors are people who lend money to a business.

Stakeholders are people who have an interest in the success of the business.

PORTFOLIO PROMPTS

Who are the stakeholders in the business you are investigating?

25 What do customers want?

Something to chew on

The Wall's ice cream factory in Gloucester is the largest manufacture of ice cream in Europe. The company has high standards of health and safety to safeguard its product. However, in a recent case, environmental health officers received a complaint from a member of the public because slivers of glass were found in a tub of Wall's ice cream. There was nothing to suggest the glass came from either the house of the customer or from the factory. Wall's offered the customer £100 and a bunch of flowers.

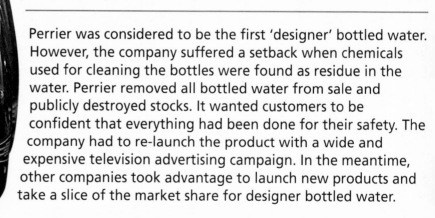

Perrier was considered to be the first 'designer' bottled water. However, the company suffered a setback when chemicals used for cleaning the bottles were found as residue in the water. Perrier removed all bottled water from sale and publicly destroyed stocks. It wanted customers to be confident that everything had been done for their safety. The company had to re-launch the product with a wide and expensive television advertising campaign. In the meantime, other companies took advantage to launch new products and take a slice of the market share for designer bottled water.

ACTION

1 Make a list of products that you buy regularly.

2 Decide what you think is the most important thing for you as a customer.

3 Look for examples in magazine or newspaper adverts of businesses setting out to meet customer needs.

IN TRAY

1 Explain the damage that Wall's may suffer if its customers are worried about a product.

2 Explain why the makers of Perrier withdrew all bottled water and publicly destroyed the contents.

3 Why did Perrier have to pay for expensive advertising to re-launch its product?

4 What did competitors do when Perrier had the problem?

5 What other stakeholders may be affected by the situation if managers do not take correct action?

Why is the customer important?

Businesses can persuade customers to buy products through good advertising. No one likes to admit that adverts alter their buying habits, but companies win millions of pounds of new orders after effective marketing campaigns.

However, if customers are worried about a product, they will not buy it. When glass was found in Wall's ice cream, the company worked hard to discover the cause. This may mean withdrawing faulty products and checking a higher number of samples to ensure the quality and safety of the product. If the customer loses confidence in the product because the company is not seen to be taking the situation seriously, sales may start to fall.

Businesses work hard to find out what their customers want. Market research is expensive and time-consuming, but it can give a business important profiles of its customers' spending habits, tastes and attitudes. Customers may feel they are having an impact on a business by filling in questionnaires and by complaining to supermarket managers and others if the products are unsatisfactory.

Customers acting together can make a difference to business behaviour. At one time, disposable nappies for babies were produced in a way which led to poisonous waste. Customers with knowledge of the environmental effects led a protest and sales began to fall. As a consequence, businesses changed their manufacturing methods.

Widespread publicity has been given to food products involving chemically modified processes. Customers have demanded more information from shops and have refused to buy certain goods. Car buyers have discovered that new cars can be bought more cheaply outside the UK. Numbers of sales of new cars at home have fallen and car companies are likely to change their prices.

Good customer care and public relations sections of businesses work hard to reassure customers with complaints.

CHECKPOINT

1 Why is the customer an important stakeholder in a business?

2 What influence does the customer have over the business?

3 Give reasons why the business should have plans to deal with possible customer complaint.

PORTFOLIO PROMPTS

Investigate your chosen local business. Who are the customers? Do they influence the actions of the business?

26 Do the staff have a stake?

OBJECTIVES

To find out how employees influence a business. .

Part of the team

Phil Taylor is sole owner of Riverside Sports and Leisure Club in Gloucester. He knows just how important the employees are to the business. The receptionist who takes the bookings must give a good first impression to the customers. The instructors must make sure that the club is friendly and relaxed so members will sign up for another year.

Phil knows that team spirit is important.

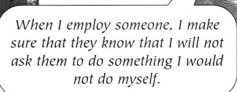

When I employ someone, I make sure that they know that I will not ask them to do something I would not do myself.

ACTION

If you managed a music store selling CDs and tapes, how would you make sure your five staff felt part of the business?

The staff can use all the facilities free of charge if they are not booked by customers. This is quite a perk, as it includes a gym, a weights room, a sauna and sun beds. If the business is doing well, staff receive a bonus. Every year there is a Christmas party for all the staff at the club.

IN TRAY

1 Why are the receptionists and instructors important to the business?

2 How does Phil encourage his staff to look after the members?

3 Why might staff find Riverside a good place to work?

4 What could Phil do to ensure that his employees stayed with his business over the next five years?

5 Customers want early morning access to the club but staff prefer later working hours. How might Phil sort out the different stakeholder interests?

Employees as active stakeholders

A positive attitude helps in any organisation. In a service industry such as a sports and leisure club, contact with customers is very important. Staff will do a better job if they feel they are part of a good organisation. In a complicated car manufacturing business, employees must work together if production is to run smoothly. Although money is an important reward, respect, praise and encouragement also motivate employees to work hard.

In some countries, the law states that employees must be involved in making decisions. A representative of the staff should be a member of the board of directors. At Nissan, for example, employees are elected to a Council, which discusses the major plans of the company.

Many businesses involve staff in other ways:

- a training and promotion scheme so everyone has a chance to move up

- suggestion boxes for staff to feed in ideas, with a prize for the best idea

- welfare and leisure activities or perks

- a scheme to share profits.

Different businesses, different stakes?

John Lewis department stores run a profit-sharing scheme which rewards employees for loyalty and long service. Pay is average for such work, but there are good additional staff benefits and social facilities.

Vamix makes mass-produced cakes and employs many young and temporary staff. The business offers a lot of work at short notice and pay can be good. There is a little staff training, but most employees stay only a short time at the factory.

IN TRAY

1 In what ways, if any, do these two businesses encourage their staff to be active stakeholders?

2 What effects do you think these different approaches might have on the success of the business?

If things go wrong?

Sometimes businesses close down or have to make people redundant. Many big companies will try to move people within the business or help them to find another job. Some may make large redundancy payments to workers who have been loyal and active stakeholders.

Employees expect a fair system to exist at work if there are complaints and problems to deal with. Businesses sometimes have to be persuaded to set up meetings and to allow groups of workers the time to meet together. Some businesses appoint managers, supervisors and workers to take responsibility for maintaining good relationships.

If problems can't be settled internally, employees may look externally to a **trade union** to help them.

KEY TERM

A **trade union** is an organisation that looks after the interests of its worker members.

PORTFOLIO PROMPTS

Put together ten questions to help you find out how employees take an active part in the business that you are investigating.

27 What about my share?

Making decisions

Chris and Amanda both own shares in a small chain of department stores. They have just received a letter about the Annual General Meeting, which tells them that there are plans to open two new stores.

> Do you know about the plans for the new stores?

> But if they don't open new stores, we'll have bigger dividends now. I bought the shares to earn me some extra money straightaway.

> Oh yes, it seems like a great idea. If the company grows, we'll get more dividends and our shares could be worth more.

> But if the company is expected to grow, some people will want to get hold of the shares and they'll be worth more.

> I'm going to go to the AGM and tell them what I think.

ACTION

Write for copies of company annual reports (these are also available on many company websites). Look for evidence in the chairman's report of the company's treatment of shareholders. What might attract you to invest in any of these companies as a shareholder?

 ## IN TRAY

1 What do Chris and Amanda both expect from their shares?

2 Explain Chris and Amanda's different points of view.

3 Why might the company pay smaller dividends now if it builds new shops?

4 Why might it pay bigger dividends later?

5 If a company doesn't pay enough to its shareholders, what might happen?

Now or later

Shareholders want a company to do well because they will get a good share of the profits through a dividend payment. If a company is not doing well, it will not be able to pay any dividends at all. If the company went bust, the shareholders would lose the money they had invested.

Shares in public companies can be bought and sold at any time. The price paid for a second-hand share depends on how well the company is doing now and how well it might do in the future. If everyone wanted to sell their shares at the same time, the **share price** would fall. If a business has a good year, there are likely to be buyers keen to get hold of shares and so their price will rise.

Up in arms

When the major shareholders of Manchester United Football Club proposed to sell their shares to a media business, many of the fans who owned shares were furious. They didn't want the ownership of the company to be sold to another business that might have different objectives for the team. They protested loudly to ensure that their point of view was heard.

IN TRAY

1   Why might a media company want a major share in Manchester United?

2   Why do you think the shareholders who were fans were worried?

3   What might the shareholders – other than the fans and the media company – want from Manchester United?

Ethical investors

Over the last ten years, many shareholders have become '**ethical' investors**. They want to know that the company in which they are investing money is

◆ offering fair conditions to its workers

◆ doing its best to care for the environment

◆ trading fairly with poorer nations

If a company has had a poor record on the environment or its treatment of employees, shareholders may sell their shares or protest at the AGM. Some directors have been voted out of office and many companies now appoint a director with responsibility for ensuring that the company behaves fairly.

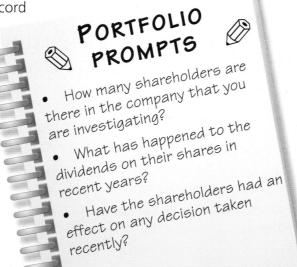

PORTFOLIO PROMPTS

• How many shareholders are there in the company that you are investigating?

• What has happened to the dividends on their shares in recent years?

• Have the shareholders had an effect on any decision taken recently?

KEY TERMS

Share price is the value of second-hand shares on the stock market.

Ethical investors are shareholders who buy shares of companies with good reputations for environmental care, fair trading etc.

28 Good neighbours

A flowering partnership

Whitbread employs 150 people at its regional headquarters in Cheltenham. It owns 3,400 pubs, Pizza Hut, Café Rouge and many other outlets.

The company's programme of work in the community covers a range of activities, from education to helping people overcome the problems of living in poor parts of the country.

The local community in Cheltenham is proud of its regional, national and European awards as an attractive town. This is important to attract the tourist trade. Whitbread recently contributed £52,000 to a flower basket campaign with the local newspaper.

As part of a national health and safety education programme, Whitbread worked with local schools to allow pupils to visit the site and to take part in training activities. The business takes pupils on work experience and helps to support vocational work for GNVQ courses. Staff sometimes visit schools and the business helps to sponsor events.

IN TRAY

1. What links does Whitbread make with the local community?
2. How do such links help local schools?
3. Why do businesses run community programmes like this?
4. How can a company justify such spending to its shareholders?

What does the community want?

The local community is an important partner for many businesses. Workers are usually local, as are some consumers of the business's products. If the business needs to expand its site, it will need the support of the community and planning permission from the local council.

The local community generally wants business to behave in a responsible manner. It does not want it to pollute the environment or create traffic congestion. People are very wary about new developments near where they live, and are often anxious about the effects on their children.

Businesses know that the community is watching the way they behave and is also looking for their help. Some businesses support the arts, while others help young people to develop and find jobs. Some work with special charities. By involving themselves in local community activities, businesses find it easier to sort out problems and to keep up good relationships. The oil company BP describes this as seeking a 'licence to operate'.

ACTION

Look in past and present editions of your local paper to see how business links with the community are reported. What have businesses done to foster a good partnership?

Say NO to the supermarket!

Sometimes there are conflicts between a business and a local community.

IN TRAY

1 What are the protesters angry about?

2 Why would a supermarket business want to open another store?

3 What might the supermarket company do to encourage local community support for the development?

Cementing good relationships

It is often when local developments are planned that the strength of the links between business and the local community are most evident. Businesses pay rates to the local council where they are based. As with any other taxpayer, a business feels entitled to a say in what is going on. A local council has responsibility for planning on behalf of the community but has to rely on the government and on business partners to finance a major part of big developments. In return for the opportunity to build a new office, a business might agree to develop a park and community facilities nearby. The national government has encouraged businesses to take part in local development by giving them free rates for a number of years.

PORTFOLIO PROMPTS

What does the business that you are investigating do to help the community?

29 A government view

Laura Ashley bids farewell

Laura Ashley, the clothes and fabric manufacturer, is closing its major factory and selling two others by the end of the year. The Wrexham factory will cost 150 jobs, while the sale of the original factories in mid-Wales will mean a tough 345 job losses for two small communities.

The company had lost over £8 million in the last six months. A Malaysian property business now owns over half of the company and hopes the future will be better. High street shops, including Laura Ashley's 300 UK and European stores, are not having a good time. Shoppers have little spare spending money and expect interest rates to rise soon.

MPs call for action

A Member of Parliament and a Member of the Welsh Assembly have called for a meeting with the Laura Ashley board to discuss the future of the Welsh factories. If the company does leave Wales, a government organisation – the Welsh Development Agency – is there to help find new businesses. (See pp. 114–5.)

We must find a new user for the Wrexham factory. Some local companies can employ Laura Ashley staff.

WDA

We can't sit by and watch businesses leave an area with very high unemployment levels. It might be possible for the government to find a way of helping the company through grants.

MP

IN TRAY

1 Why is Laura Ashley closing factories in Wales?

2 Why is this such a serious matter for the Welsh towns affected?

3 What could the government and its organisation, the WDA, do to help the situation?

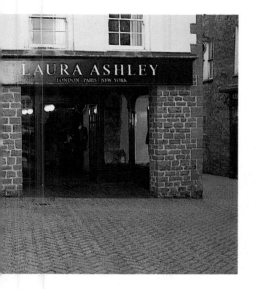

Governments have an interest

Governments don't make a habit of helping out businesses directly. If a business loses money, it is a problem for the owners and managers. But it is good for a country to have successful firms. Areas of the country with high levels of unemployment need new help to redevelop. Government finances benefit too, because workers are in jobs, pay taxes and don't need unemployment pay. The government has a 'stake' in the decisions taken by Laura Ashley.

The government may be able to help Laura Ashley by encouraging trade deals between businesses in the UK and Malaysia. If the Malaysian owners see that business is going well, they may be in a better position to finance Laura Ashley's recovery.

The government can also encourage consumers to spend more in the shops. This can be done indirectly by cutting taxes, or keeping **interest** rates down so that loans are cheaper.

There are always difficult choices for governments to make. Should precious funds be spent helping Laura Ashley employees or on other important projects such as the building of new hospitals?

... tax cuts

... jobs saved in factory

... more spending

... more orders for Laura Ashley

Governments have a legal stake too

The government makes laws on behalf of the whole community and expects business to play its part in putting them into practice. A good business will show the way on fair treatment of workers, careful waste disposal and the maintenance of dangerous equipment, including large lorries. Some businesses try to cut corners and the government has to take action. Typical examples include:

- fines for pollution of local rivers and discharge of dangerous gases
- inspection of factories by health and safety teams
- investigations of unfair price fixing to overcharge customers
- prosecution in the courts for running unsafe vehicles.

CHECKPOINT

1 Some government help takes time to have an effect. Why would this be a problem for Laura Ashley?

2 A grant to keep open a Laura Ashley factory for two years or a new hospital in Manchester. Which project would you support with limited government money? Why?

3 In what other ways do you think a government could help businesses?

4 Why do you think the government has felt it necessary to pass consumer protection laws?

PORTFOLIO PROMPTS

Find out about any laws that apply to the business you are investigating. What effect have these laws had on the way the business operates?

KEY TERM

Interest is money charged by a lender for the use of their money.

151

30 Pressure groups

OBJECTIVES
To find out about the role of pressure groups as stakeholders in business.

Battle goes on at St James's site

In the centre of Cheltenham is the site of the old St James's station. The local council, in partnership with several large stores, has a plan to develop the site by building a big shopping centre. The development plan also includes a large leisure centre with cinema and bowling alley on a nearby site. This project will create 800 jobs for the Cheltenham area.

Many local residents prefer to see more housing rather than shops. They have formed a pressure group to argue for a housing development. The pressure group has taken action.

◆ It has delivered leaflets and invited everyone to protest.

◆ It has asked archaeologists to research the site and so delay the building work.

◆ 30 'Eco-warriors' have set up a treetop camp in land threatened by the development.

Fitzgerald Castle

Fitzgerald Castle is a stately home in the country. Part of it is already open to the public, and it attracts tourists daily. The castle's owner plans a £2 million development, which will attract an extra 100,000 people to the local village of Ballycodley every year.

Angry residents have formed an action group. They say that they have not been consulted and will fight the plans. They think the development will threaten local businesses and cause traffic congestion. A resident said, 'We're talking about quality of life. We've the pleasure of enjoying Ballycodley as it is and as it should stay'.

IN TRAY

1 What do local residents want in Cheltenham and in Ballycodley?

2 What action have local residents in Ballycodley taken to make sure their views are heard?

3 What are the advantages in joining together with others as a pressure group?

4 What decision do you think will be best for Cheltenham and for Ballycodley? Why?

Pressure group opposition

A business may need to update and expand to keep its customers. It may face opposition from **pressure groups** for many reasons. Local communities set up groups to preserve their way of life and to safeguard their rights. We can see this may cause a conflict of interest. Employment, housing and environmental issues are important.

The local council planning office has to take into account the opinions of many people who have an interest in the area. It gives planning permission and influences developments. Residents' protests have to be investigated and an enquiry can take years to complete.

Pressure groups may be local – like the Friends of Ballycodley – national or international. Some of the big groups, like Greenpeace, are very powerful. They communicate their views by getting the attention of the media. Many businesses have learnt that they need to work hand in hand with such pressure groups instead of fighting them.

ACTION

Look for reports in your local paper about local groups taking action or arguing for or against change. How many of these groups are protesting about business activities?

Extending jobs or noise?

Staverton is a small local airport in Gloucester. It is used by a range of businesses, including air taxi operations, private and commercial pilot training, crop spraying and dusting, and recreational and sports flying.

The number of passengers on regular flights has declined since 1993 and an air tour operator, Aeroscope Travel, believes the only solution is to extend the runway to allow larger jets to use the airport.

Aeroscope employs about 30 people and charters planes for passengers to fly to Jersey and Guernsey. The main debate has been about safety and noise legislation.

IN TRAY

1 What benefits might the extended runway bring to the local area?

2 What objections would you make as a local resident?

3 A planning inspector would need to hear evidence from everyone involved in the development. What information do you think would be important in making the final decision?

PORTFOLIO PROMPTS

Write a summary about a pressure group of your choice. Give examples of the strategies the group uses to put pressure on the business.

KEY TERM

Pressure group is a group of like-minded people who join together to try to influence decisions taken by businesses, councils and the government.

1 Money makes the world go round

Remember Just Micro?

Ian Stewart set up Just Micro to sell computer games. He needed to borrow money from the bank in order to start the business, so he had to make careful plans.

The plans had to show all the costs involved in running the business and an estimate of how much it would earn. It also had to show that Ian had thought about all the activities that are involved in running a business. The bank would then decide whether the proposal was sensible and if the business would make a profit.

 IN TRAY

1 What costs did Ian have to take into account in his plan?

2 What other information do you think the bank manager would want to see in the business plan?

3 Why is it important to keep a check on the money that is going in and out of a business?

ACTION

How do you control your income and expenditure? Ask someone you know who is working how he or she goes about it.

Planning ahead

Whatever a business makes or does, it always has to plan.

◆ A new business must make a business plan for the bank if it wants to borrow money.

◆ A business that wants to sell a new product must make a plan to show that the sales will be high enough to make a profit.

◆ A business that wants to expand must show that the scheme will work.

All these plans will show the costs and revenues which are expected from the business. The plan for a new business will take into account the choice of location, staff and marketing as well as the resources and equipment which are needed to make the products.

Whatever a business is planning, it must:

◆ know how much to produce in order to break even

◆ ensure that there is enough cash to cover the bills

◆ balance the accounts

◆ work out the profit or loss.

The finance team

Sunderland football club employs a team of people to look after the finances. They must keep records of all the money that comes in and all that goes out of the club. This ensures that the club does not get into difficulties.

Some of the staff work on wages, others work on ticket sales and looking after the supporters' shops. Money comes from all sorts of sources and has to be paid out to many people.

The club has different financial systems that help it to keep control. In one year, the club's turnover is £18.9 million, so it is a major task.

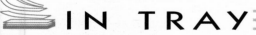

IN TRAY

1 Look back to pages 36–7 to remind yourself where Sunderland's money comes from.

2 What does the club spend money on?

3 Why is it so important to monitor the flow of money?

4 How can a computer help?

Any business must have systems that help it to control the money in the organisation. In a small business these systems will be simple, but a computer is often helpful.

In a big business information from many departments must be fed into the system, so it is more complex. All this information contributes to the accounting processes.

The finance department is usually responsible for monitoring the company's progress so that there are no nasty surprises. In a large organisation it can be easy for spending to be greater than income if controls are not in place.

In small and medium-sized businesses a standard computer package can be used to monitor activity. Very large organisations will need a specially designed system to meet their needs.

2 Lighting the fuse

This must sell!

Did you know that Cadbury's is the world's fourth-largest seller of sweets and chocolates? It sells chocolates in 165 countries – in fact, nearly everywhere in the world. How can the business possibly make sure that its sales stay this big?

One way to keep sales healthy is to produce a new snack bar. Cadbury's Dairy Milk bars have been on sale since 1905. They still sell well, but when the business wanted to sell more it needed a new product.

Cadbury's has four objectives:

♦ To be the **market leader** – that means having the biggest sales

♦ To increase the quantity of chocolate products it can sell

♦ To break into new markets

♦ To keep ahead of the competition.

IN TRAY

1	Why would Cadbury's want to sell more snack bars?
2	What would it need to do in order to produce and sell a new snack bar?

ACTION

Find out what kind of snack bars are bought by each member of your class. Find out for each person which is their favourite and draw up a table ranking the most popular brands. Which one do you think is advertised the most? Is this the favourite?

Starting to sell a new product takes much careful preparation. Every business needs to be sure of:

♦ being able to sell the product
♦ selling at a price that covers the costs.

Many decisions must be taken. Look at the flow chart. The most important question is the first one. The business must make a product that customers really want. But it must do it in a way which costs less than the price it can charge.

What sort of chocolate bar would customers like most?	→	Who will want to buy the product?	→	How will the product be made?	→	How much will it cost to produce?	→	What price will people pay?	→	Is this price higher than the cost?

The answer to the last question in the flowchart has to be yes! If it is no, it would be better to stop right there and not make the product at all.

What Cadbury's did

First, the market research team found out an important fact through secondary research:

◆ 16–34 year olds buy more than one-third of all sweets and chocolates sold. The product needed to attract this age group.

Next, the team carried out primary research to find out more about what people would like. This is what it found out:

◆ Cadbury's needed a chocolate bar with special qualities, different from competing products.

◆ It must combine chocolate with other ingredients to give the bar a new texture.

◆ It must make the packaging exciting and different.

Using this market research, Cadbury's came up with a mixture of raisins, cereal, peanuts and fudge pieces 'fused' together with chocolate to make a bar. It used a bright logo to give the bar its own personality.

What Cadbury's spent

It took five years to do the market research and develop the product. Cadbury's built a new factory near Bristol. In all, it spent £40 million just getting the product to the market. Then it spent £4 million on advertising.

LAUNCHING A NEW PRODUCT INTO A DEVELOPED MARKET

THE TIMES 100
1997/8

IN TRAY

1 What was the total cost of market research, setting up the factory and launching the Fuse bar?

2 Explain how Cadbury's used the marketing mix to make the Fuse bar sell.

3 Why did Cadbury's think it was worth spending so much money on its plans for the Fuse bar?

Cadbury's asked itself all the questions in the flow diagram. It made quite sure that this product was what customers wanted. Then it made quite sure that as many people as possible would want it. Cadbury's promoted the Fuse bar as hard as it could.

Because 85 per cent of all new processed foods fail within the first year of production, Cadbury's worked very hard in order to be certain of success. The business thought it was worth spending a lot of money to avoid the risk of the Fuse bar being a flop.

KEY TERM

A **market leader** is the business with the biggest sales compared to competing businesses.

157

3 What are the costs?

OBJECTIVES

To examine the costs and revenues involved in starting to sell a new product.

To consider how costs and revenues affect business decisions.

What happened on Fuseday?

Cadbury's knew it had to be sure that retailers and wholesalers liked the Fuse bar, otherwise it would not even appear in the shops. It provided briefings for retailers and distributors and sent out colourful displays to highlight Fuse bars on the shelves.

New snack bars are often given a local trial, but Cadbury's felt confident enough to launch Fuse nationally. The bar was launched on 24 September 1996, a day which Cadbury's named 'Fuseday'. A total of 40 million Fuse bars had been sent to the Cadbury wholesale depots and distributors all over the UK were ready to launch the product. Press releases told the story of how it had been developed, while television ads made certain everyone knew about it.

Within three months, Fuse had:

◆   sold 70 million bars

◆   sold more than Mars or KitKat

◆   got 6.5 per cent of the market for snack bars

◆   helped the overall chocolate market to grow by 19 per cent.

A few weeks after the launch, surveys showed that most people had heard of the Fuse bar and recognised the brand name.

The Fuse bar did well because Cadbury's co-ordinated its marketing and product development efforts. It aimed for high sales, matched the product to customer preferences and spent freely on promotion.

 PORTFOLIO PROMPTS

Has the business that you are investigating launched a new product? List both the start-up costs and the running costs and provide figures if possible. Or you may be part of a mini-enterprise. (If you are not, you may know someone who is.) If you are, you will have had to think about the start-up costs of your business. Explain how you try to make sure that both sorts of costs can be covered.

 IN TRAY

1   Make a list of all the inputs needed by Cadbury's to make the Fuse bar.

2   Retailers usually pay about 20p each to the wholesale for the Fuse bars they buy in bulk. If Cadbury's got 15p from the wholesaler, how much money did it make from Fuse bar sales in the first three months?

3   How did this compare with what Cadbury's had already spent?

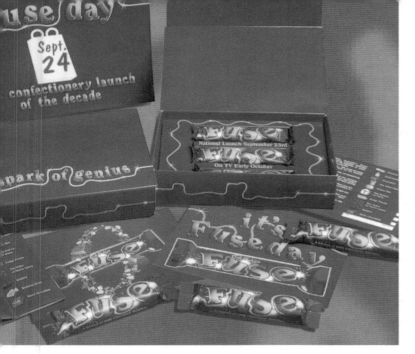

Some of the costs of the Fuse bar were **start-up costs**, which covered all the things that had to be done before the product was ready for the market. Many of Cadbury's start-up costs for the Fuse bar were explained on the last page. The high start-up costs were essential to the success of the product. Cadbury's was able to spend large sums in this way because it is a very big business with many well-established products.

Other inputs are needed to keep production going. These are the **running costs**. All sorts of different people are needed to keep the factory operating and to get the Fuse bars to the shops. The spider diagram shows these costs.

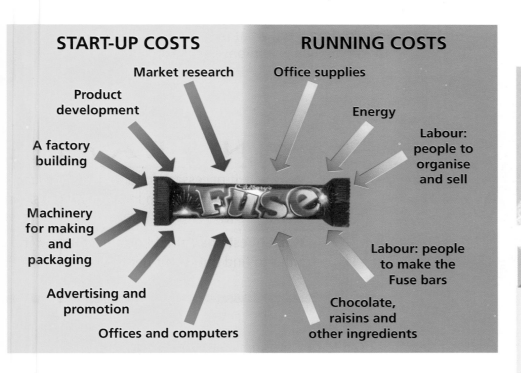

START-UP COSTS

Market research

Product development

A factory building

Machinery for making and packaging

Advertising and promotion

Offices and computers

RUNNING COSTS

Office supplies

Energy

Labour: people to organise and sell

Labour: people to make the Fuse bars

Chocolate, raisins and other ingredients

Sales revenue

Once sales start, money begins to come in. Every time a Fuse bar sells, Cadbury's receive a price for it. The money from all sales put together is called **sales revenue**. A growing market means higher sales revenue, simply because more people are buying. This makes it easier to cover the high start-up costs.

Sales revenue can be calculated quite easily with this formula:

$$\text{Price} \times \text{quantity sold} = \text{sales revenue}$$

CHECKPOINT

Not all the costs Cadbury's had to cover when producing the Fuse bar have been included in the spider diagram. What other costs can you think of? Say which are start-up costs and which are running costs.

KEY TERMS

⟁ **Start-up costs** have to be paid for all the inputs that are needed before sales can be made. They include market research and buildings and machinery which are bought.

⟁ **Running costs** have to be paid for all the inputs needed to keep production going.

⟁ **Sales revenue** is all the money that comes in from the sale of the product. It is the price times the amount sold.

4 Dreaming of business

How do you know what will sell?

Linda wanted to open a new beauty therapy business in the small shopping precinct near her home. How could she find out whether there would be enough demand for this type of service?

She decided to ask the women who lived in the houses and flats nearby if they would use a beauty therapist. She drew up a list of questions to ask.

A friend suggested that she should look in the local telephone directories to see how many other beauty therapy salons there were in town, then find out where they were, using a map. Linda would not want to be too close to another beauty therapy salon. She also found out what prices other salons charged for facials, nail extensions and waxing.

IN TRAY

1   Why was it necessary for Linda to find out whether the people who live around her salon would use it?

2   What questions would Linda need to ask in order to find out about her market?

Market research is used to get information that the business does not already have. By carrying out market research Linda will find out about who her customers are likely to be and what types of product they will want.

Market research gathers information about the following:

◆   the size of the market

◆   the type of customer who will buy the product

◆   where the customers are

◆   what types of products will sell

◆   who the main competitors will be

◆   what prices to charge.

What Linda found out

Linda found that there were women who were already customers of other beauty therapists who might be interested in coming to her salon, as it would be nearer. She found a few people who showed a general interest and might become customers in the long run. Then Linda began to worry. She thought the next thing she should do was to work out all the costs she would have to cover before the business could open.

She found out the cost of renting the shop she wanted and the cost of fitting it with the minimum of equipment. She priced a couch, trolley, magnifier, wax heater, nail extension equipment, overalls and two chairs. Then she thought about her own time. She thought that if she charged £20 an hour for the time spent with customers, she would be able to cover her costs.

IN TRAY

1   Why is it important to cost all the items needed before deciding whether to start a business?

2   How can Linda be sure that customers will be prepared to pay £20 per hour?

3   Linda still hasn't really thought out her plans properly. What has she left out of her list of costs? Has she made other mistakes?

4   Linda is thinking through her plans in the same way that Cadbury's did when it planned the Fuse bar. What are the differences between the way Linda does this and the way Cadbury's did it?

3   Linda carried out both primary and secondary market research. List all the research she did and say which was primary and which was secondary.

ACTION

Imagine you are opening a new business. In small groups, work out what your product will be and design a questionnaire that would help you to decide how the business should be set up. Make sure you find out the following information:

◆ what possible customers most want you to sell

◆ the age groups of your likely customers

◆ how often they would buy from you

Design a recording sheet that will make the collection of results easy. You could use a spreadsheet for this. Ask 10 people your questions and produce a chart to show the results.

5 Reality

A better plan

Linda realised that the business idea she was thinking about was really too ambitious. She could not be sure that she would have enough customers to cover her costs. She decided against the shop in the local precinct. Her front room wasn't getting much use, so she decided to turn it into a salon. She would have to pay **business rates** to the local council, but she would save the rent on the shop.

This time she listed her start-up costs and her running costs properly. Linda already had the prices she had found for her original plan and she got an estimate from a firm of decorators for painting the room. She costed all the items such as towels, telephone bills, heating and electricity that she had forgotten before. She included the make-up and cotton wool pads, cleansing fluids, couch rolls, oils for massage and wax treatment materials. She remembered that she would need insurance, in case anything ever went wrong.

Linda decided to stay with her price of £20 per hour, which would have to cover all her costs. She thought about one-third of it would be needed to cover all the inputs for particular treatments. Then she would have to allow something to cover her start-up costs.

Finally, Linda thought about what kind of promotion would be needed. She realised this could be quite costly too.

IN TRAY

1 Which of the costs that Linda has thought of are running costs and which are start-up costs?

2 What will happen if she gets only enough customers to work about half-time? What will happen to her costs? What will happen to her sales revenue?

3 What new costs might she have to cover in the future?

ACTION

To be successful, Beautiful Trends had to compete with other similar businesses. In a small group, make a list of all the things that might help Linda to compete. Discuss which of these will be the most important.

Many new businesses fail because they have not made careful plans. Starting a new business is risky, but keeping costs under control reduces some of the risk. By setting up in her own home, Linda was avoiding paying rent and making it more likely that her business would survive. She also saved the cost of fitting the new shop, which would have added greatly to her start-up costs.

As well as thinking about costs, it is important to think about sales revenue. If the business has a good plan for advertising its product, it is likely to sell more and revenue will be higher.

Small businesses need to consider advertising in local papers. Sometimes feature articles promote the businesses in the local area. Special offers can be displayed inside a shop. People can be encouraged to introduce a friend. These are all inexpensive ways of marketing the product which are practical for small businesses.

Bigger businesses such as Cadbury's can afford to advertise in national newspapers and on TV. With high sales, the cost is spread over a large quantity of output.

Beautiful Trends

As Linda became more confident, she realised that she needed a good name for the business. When she was nearly ready to open for business, she designed a leaflet advertising what she could offer and delivered it herself to all the homes nearby. Soon after she started she found she was getting customers through personal recommendations. After a while, she realised that this was for her really the most important way to get business. She began to target her best customers with special offers.

Beautiful Trends
- Body massage
- Waxing
- Facials
- Bridal make-up
- Makeovers
- Eyebrow shaping

GIFT TOKENS AVAILABLE

5 Glenthorn Road
Bonnington
St Andrews

Telephone
(0107) 87630

IN TRAY

1   Is advertising a start-up or a running cost?

2   What will happen to a business which does not advertise much?

KEY TERM

Business rates are taxes paid to the local council by businesses. They help to pay for the services provided by the council, for example streets and street lighting, refuse collection and police.

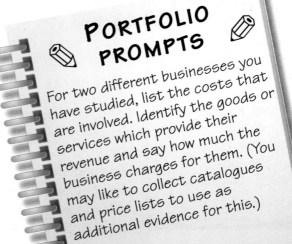

PORTFOLIO PROMPTS

For two different businesses you have studied, list the costs that are involved. Identify the goods or services which provide their revenue and say how much the business charges for them. (You may like to collect catalogues and price lists to use as additional evidence for this.)

6 Rent or buy?

Silver Linings Ltd

Mike Bassett had been working for some time in an insurance brokers in Brighton. He advised customers on where to find the best deals for their house and car insurance policies. He could always tell customers if they would be paying a lower premium by switching to another insurance company.

After seven years, Mike felt he could offer a better, more personal, service if he set up on his own. He went to see estate agents about office space.

He found he could buy a single small office in a back street for £15,000. He would need to make a down payment of £2,000. The rest would come from a **mortgage**, which would cost about £33 a week if he paid it off in ten years. He knew this might be risky.

Alternatively, he could get two small offices on the first floor over a shop in a town-centre location for £45 per week (£2,300 per year). They had night storage heaters, carpets and good lighting. The **lease** was for three years but could be renewed.

IN TRAY

1 Why might someone starting up on their own rent their premises?

2 What other overhead costs would Mike have to cover?

3 How could Mike be sure he would be able to pay the rent or the mortgage when he first started in business?

4 Which of the two properties do you think Mike would choose?

5 How will Mike's start-up costs be affected by his decision?

ACTION

Ask one person who is in business in your area whether they own or rent their premises, and why. Write down the answer and in groups of three, compare your findings.

Renting an office, a shop or even a factory building makes sense for many businesses because changes can be made fairly easily. The business will be given a lease, which runs for several years. If it needs larger premises it may be able to rent more space in the same building.

Of course, buying premises gives the business much more control. It can plan its space, make alterations freely and stay in the same place for a long time.

If the business rents its premises, the rent will be a running cost. However, if the business buys its premises, any down payment and legal costs will be start-up costs. But it will end up owning the building.

Do you want the best deal you can get for your car insurance?

Come to Silver Linings

You'll never look back...

Tel: 0226 785934

IN TRAY

1   List the advantages of renting and the advantages of buying premises for Silver Linings.

2   Why do you think Mike might want to buy this time?

Silver Linings expands

Offering a personal advice service worked well for Mike. The business grew and he took on more staff. Before long, the offices became very crowded. Mike managed to rent the rooms next door, and then he took on staff who could work from home.

Next he hit on the idea of offering his services on the Internet. He began to take business from all over the country. He needed new, much bigger premises, fast.

Mike looked around and found a bigger office property, which he could rent for £22,000 a year. Alternatively, he could buy the place for £240,000. That would mean he could design the inside to suit his requirements. He would need a mortgage so he could pay for it over a period of years. He worked out that the mortgage would be very close to the cost of the rent, if he borrowed all of the money needed. He thought he would be able to pay partly in cash, as he had some savings.

PORTFOLIO PROMPTS

Think about a particular type of business that you could set up in your area. Work out what sort of premises you would need. Find out what is available and could be suitable. Compare the rent with the revenue you think you could earn. This could be part of a business plan.

7 Out on the town

Jemz

Judi, Rachael, Tim and James wanted to set up and run a nightclub in Newton Abbott in Devon. They set to work to make a **business plan**. They could contribute £80,000 from their own savings, but they would have to borrow the rest or find other businesses that would be willing to back them. They decided to work as a partnership.

Their market research showed that people over 18 would pay £5 per night. They could offer an under-18s night to increase revenue with a lower ticket price. They planned to charge more for both drinks and admission after 11 p.m. The next nearest nightclubs were quite a long way off, so they would face very little competition. Their target market was everyone aged 17 to 40 who lived within a 20-mile radius.

They found a good town-centre site for the club. The building had been a garage, but it had closed down. It was very reasonably priced at £80,000, which they could pay with their own savings. They worked out the cost of renovation and fittings for the building, which was soundly constructed but derelict. Air conditioning, furniture and music equipment would also be needed.

They estimated their sales revenue and running costs for the first year – these are shown in Figure 1. The cost of refitting the premises came to £500,000, which would have to be borrowed. The loan repayment and interest would come to £180,667 in the first year.

Figure 1 Estimated sales revenue and running costs, Year 1

	£
Sales revenue	
Admission charges	521,842
Drink sales	1,420,900
Total income	1,942,742
	£
Running costs	
Drinks	710,450
Wages	166,660
Salaries	31,200
Telephone	260
Electricity	2,080
Heating	2,600
Licences	132
Total costs	913,382

IN TRAY

1 How much **profit** did the Jemz team expect to make?

2 Estimate how long it would take the team to pay back their loan.

3 What were the risks involved in this plan?

A **business plan** has to show how the business will work. It must cover marketing plans, production costs and how it will be financed. There must be some evidence of market research to show that the estimates of sales revenue are realistic. All the inputs must be carefully costed. It must convince the bank or any other backer that the business is likely to be successful.

The plan will also need to be able to show that the people setting up the business have the skills they will need. All of the Jemz team were studying business, so they understood what was required. What they did not have was real experience of running a business.

Jemz

What happened next

The Jemz team presented their plan to the bank manager. They estimated that they would be able to pay the bank back within two years. They told the bank manager that they knew it would be impossible to have a loan for the full amount, but they asked for her advice.

The bank manager was very impressed. The detail in their report seemed to cover everything they could possibly think of, and she complimented them on their efforts. Then she explained that the bank expected its customers to put up at least one-third of the cost of setting up the business. She suggested the following course of action:

♦ going over the start-up costs to see if some could be cut

♦ looking for a backer, possibly someone already operating nightclubs in other areas, who would put up a large slice of the money.

She was quite clear that she could not support the team with any kind of loan until they had other sources of finance.

IN TRAY

1 What evidence was there that the team were being rather optimistic?

2 What would happen to the profits from the nightclub?

ACTION

In a small group, put yourselves in the position of a possible backer for the nightclub. What questions would you want to ask? Assuming that you have some money, would you be interested or does the plan look too risky?

KEY TERMS

○╼ A **business plan** is a report which explains how a new business will market its product, what it will cost to produce and how much money will be needed to start up the business.

○╼ **Profit** is the difference between sales revenue and costs.

8 Success at last!

Beautiful Trends sells well

Working from her front room, Linda did well. She created a welcoming atmosphere in her salon and customers came to her through word-of-mouth contacts.

In time, she found she was often booked up several days ahead and could not do anything for people calling at short notice. She wanted to take on an assistant, but there was nowhere for her to work. She also wanted to offer a wider range of services, but she had nowhere to put the necessary equipment.

Linda started to think again about having a shop in the precinct. She went to look at a vacant shop, which was for rent at £90 per week. There were two rooms, but they needed decorating and a reception area would have to be created. She asked a business specialising in shopfitting for an estimate for what she needed. When she added up the cost of all the fittings and equipment, it came to £9,500. That meant asking the bank for a loan.

The small business adviser told Linda to come back when she had made a business plan.

IN TRAY

1 Explain what Linda must do in order to begin writing her business plan.

2 Explain why Linda had to have a plan before the bank would lend her money.

3 How would costs and revenues be affected by the move to the precinct?

PORTFOLIO PROMPTS

Write a business plan for a product that could be provided locally by a small business.

ACTION

Put Linda's costs and revenues on two spreadsheets. One will show her costs and revenues now, while she is working from home. The other will estimate her costs and revenues after she has moved to the shop and taken on her assistant.

The purpose of a business plan is to explain the direction that the business will follow. It can help the bank to decide whether a loan should be given, and it can also help the business to organise itself. The plan will need to state clearly:

Beautiful Trends

5 Glenthorn Road
Bonnington
St Andrews

Telephone
(0107) 87630

◆ the objectives for the business (both long-term and short-term)

◆ the resources required

◆ the plans for working methods, sales and marketing

◆ the legal and insurance requirements of the business

◆ how the business will grow and develop

◆ how the business will be financed.

Banks have small business advisers who help people to draw up a business plan. Linda explained to the banker that she had trained as a beauty therapist at college and had always wanted to start her own business. She provided a lot of detail on how Beautiful Trends worked.

The business plan

Working from home, Linda had been booked on average about 30 hours a week. She spent the rest of her time doing the accounts and ordering supplies. She decided to stick to her pricing system of £20 per hour. Each week, she spent £200 on supplies of cosmetics and other inputs.

Now she was planning to recruit an assistant, who would work for £7 an hour for 15 hours a week. That would mean that Linda's input costs would rise in proportion.

Linda used this information to calculate her likely profit in the shop. She said in her plan that she had saved £6,000 towards the cost of refitting the shop. The bank read her plan and immediately said that they would give her a loan for the rest of the cost. They also offered her **overdraft** facilities while she built up the business. They suggested that she would need to do more to promote her products if she wanted to attract more customers.

IN TRAY

1 Are there any other costs which Linda will need to estimate for her business plan?

2 Write a short mission statement that will help the bank to understand Linda's objectives. (No more than three sentences.)

3 Why did Linda succeed in getting a bank loan while the Jemz team failed?

KEY TERM

⊙━ⁿ An **overdraft** allows a business to borrow from the bank to pay expenses that cannot be covered by sales revenue immediately but could be in the near future. The business borrows only the amount actually needed. The bank will allow borrowing up to the maximum agreed.

9 White knuckles

OBJECTIVES

To explore the importance of matching the product to the market so that revenue is as high as possible.

To think about the way promotion and prices affect both sales and revenue.

Theme parks grow

Alton Towers is a theme park in Staffordshire which provides a whole range of experiences. Some rides target small children and their parents; bigger rides thrill and scare. Trains and aerial rides take customers across the park to its different areas. Every year, 2.7 million people visit Alton Towers. If there were any more visitors, there would be overcrowding and long queues, so the theme park's managers do not actually want to attract more people. However, they do want to:

◆ increase the amount people spend when they visit through sales of food and drink

◆ make sure they come again next year.

This means that they must think of ways to increase customer satisfaction. One way to do this is to introduce new rides, so that people who come again can have a different experience. White knuckle rides – the exciting ones like Nemesis and Oblivion – are very popular and appeal especially to the youth market. New family rides have also been introduced.

The park has an inclusive entrance price, so that the cost of the day is known in advance and customers do not have to pay for each individual ride. There is a ticket system for the most popular rides, so that a place can be reserved and other rides enjoyed, rather than queuing. This, too, has increased customer satisfaction.

IN TRAY

1 Why does Alton Towers work so hard to achieve customer satisfaction?

2 The entry ticket for Alton Towers in 1999 was £15.50 for under-14s and £19.50 for age 14 and above. Families paid £59. Would it make sense for Alton Towers to reduce the price to attract more visitors? Give your reasons.

3 How can Alton Towers increase revenue in the future?

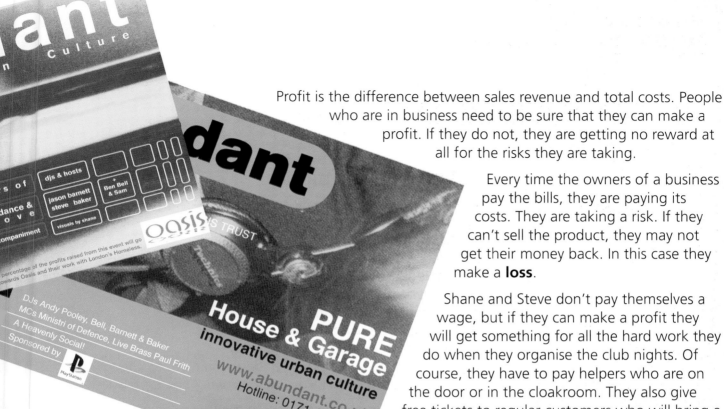

Profit is the difference between sales revenue and total costs. People who are in business need to be sure that they can make a profit. If they do not, they are getting no reward at all for the risks they are taking.

Every time the owners of a business pay the bills, they are paying its costs. They are taking a risk. If they can't sell the product, they may not get their money back. In this case they make a **loss**.

Shane and Steve don't pay themselves a wage, but if they can make a profit they will get something for all the hard work they do when they organise the club nights. Of course, they have to pay helpers who are on the door or in the cloakroom. They also give free tickets to regular customers who will bring a number of friends with them. These don't appear as a cost in the accounts.

Did Steve count everything?

After Abundant's first club night, Steve made out the accounts you saw on the opposite page. However, he quickly realised that he had left out all the overheads. They had used lighting equipment and Playstations which Shane had just bought. They had also used their own records. The cost of sending out promotion cards had been left out, too.

The mailing had included a number of other events. Altogether it had cost £950 to design, print and post the cards. Steve decided to allow £225 towards the cost of the mailing in his accounts for the club night. In the same way, he allowed £150 for the cost of their own sound and Playstation equipment. He decided not to cost the records for now. For the lighting system he allowed £100.

IN TRAY

1 How much did these extra costs come to?

2 Allowing for these extra costs, what profit did Abundant make on the club night?

3 If you were Steve or Shane, would you be pleased with the profit?

KEY TERMS

Accounts show the money received and the money spent by a business.

A **loss** is made if costs are higher than the sales revenue.

Overheads are the costs that have to be paid anyway and are separate from the costs of creating the product itself.

11 An Abundant year

OBJECTIVES

To investigate how profits are calculated over the year.

To see how businesses change over time.

Abundant gets bigger

Although Shane and Steve didn't make much money out of Abundant, they began to run more events and enjoyed the business. Besides club nights, they ran a boat party, which involved hiring a boat and partying up and down the River Thames. They also decided to offer two snowboarding holidays. Club members would get to know each other better – and perhaps the holidays would be profitable.

Shane negotiated deals with the travel company Chrystal, getting a **discount** because the customers would be looked after on the trip by Abundant's own tour directors.

The two sides of the business worked well. People who came to the club nights knew some of the people they would be holidaying with. Holiday reunion club nights were well attended.

At the end of the year Shane and Steve realised they needed an accountant to draw up the accounts for the year. The accountant added together all the club night costs but detailed the overhead costs. These are shown in Figure 1.

CHECKPOINT

1 What would Shane and Steve need to do if they wanted to decide whether holidays were more profitable than club nights?

2 Which of its 1997 expenses represented items which Abundant could carry on using in 1998? How might this affect the 1998 accounts?

Figure 1

	1997
Sales revenue	£20,183
Cost of club nights and holiday packages	£12,404
Expenses	
Travel	£549
Postage	£2,228
Telephone	£228
Stationery (leaflets)	£732
Records and equipment	£1,548
Office equipment	£1,446
Professional fees (accountant)	£785
Bank charges	£174
	£7,690

IN TRAY

1 How much profit did Abundant make in 1997?

2 Why were postage and stationery so expensive?

3 How do you think Shane and Steve would feel about the figures?

The advantage of annual accounts is that the business can review its progress over the year. It may be able to plan ways of cutting costs or increasing sales revenue. Either approach could help to increase profits.

Although Abundant was easily able to survive, it didn't seem to be very profitable. Shane and Steve enjoyed their holidays, but they had to work quite hard dealing with customers' problems.

Trouble ahead?

Jazz Sounds, a small recording company, sent ten of its employees on an Abundant snowboarding holiday in France as a bonus for their hard work. Shane managed to negotiate payment in stages, but in the end the company still owed Abundant £1,000 long after the holiday was over. This had a serious effect on the business's sales figures. Money that might have been profit simply didn't come in. Because Shane and Steve knew the people at Jazz Sounds well, they had thought they could safely offer **credit**.

IN TRAY

1 Shane and Steve had good daytime jobs. Could they have given them up and lived off Abundant's profits?

2 Why is it important for the people running a business to understand their costs and revenues?

3 What could they do to make the business more profitable?

abundantsnow

CHAMONIX 2000. 25/03-2000 TO 8/4-2000

KEY TERMS

A **discount** means a cut in price given to a good customer.

Credit means that the customer is allowed to pay later for goods and services they are buying now.

ACTION

The start-up costs for a business like Abundant are quite low. Working in groups of three, find one business each which the owners run from home. Local papers often carry advertising for small businesses, or you may have a neighbour who works from home. Then write a short report that explains what the products are and compares the three different businesses.

12 Playing well

Selling Manchester United

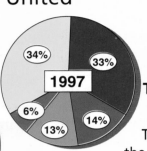

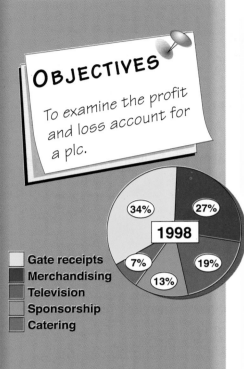

- ☐ Gate receipts
- ■ Merchandising
- ▨ Television
- ☐ Sponsorship
- ▨ Catering

	1998
	£000s
Sales revenue	£87,875
Gate receipts and programme sales	£29,778
Television	£16,203
Sponsorship	£11,771
Conferences and catering	£6,046
Merchandise sales	£24,077

Turnover analysis

Manchester United is a plc (public limited company). That means it must publish its accounts every year. All the information on these two pages comes from the Annual Report and Accounts, which anyone can obtain.

Manchester United gets income in several different ways. Television rights provide income. **Sponsorship** income grew because of a new contract with Sharp. **Merchandise** sales show the revenue from selling kit, strips, magazines and so on.

IN TRAY

1 How did Manchester United get most of its sales revenue?

2 What would it do with the revenue it received?

3 Why is it important for the business to keep its sales revenue at or above this level?

4 How might revenue from merchandise sales affect the price of tickets?

The **profit and loss account** shows sales revenue and various costs. It also shows different ways of calculating profit. Figure 1 shows the number of employees and all the costs for Manchester United, while Figure 2 shows the profit and loss account.

Figure 1 Manchester United: staff and costs

Staff	People	Expenses	£000
Players	46	Cost of sales	21,637
Ground staff	49		
Ticket office	20	Overheads	
Catering	122	Accounting services	129
Merchandising	127	Staff costs	26,897
Administration	99	Other costs	12,216

Cost of sales means the cost of making the actual product that will be sold. Manchester United includes under cost of sales the cost of buying all the merchandise that is sold in the shops and at matches. The more it sells, the more it will cost to replace its stocks.

Figure 2 Profit and loss, year ended 31 July 1998

	1998
	£000
Sales revenue	87,875
Less Cost of sales	21,637
Gross profit	66,238
Less Overheads	39,242
Net profit	26,996

The profit and loss account starts with sales revenue, then the cost of sales is subtracted to give **gross profit**. Next, overheads are subtracted. These include all the costs that must be paid just to remain in business. Overheads will stay the same however much of the product is sold. That leaves **net profit**. This is an important figure because shareholders will use it to tell them how well the company is performing.

Manchester United includes all its staff costs as overheads or expenses. In fact, the largest part of overheads is the wages and salaries paid to staff.

Out of its net profit, Manchester United will need to pay interest on its loans. Then it may decide to buy some new players, which will mean paying transfer fees. Tax will have to be paid, too. The rest of the profit can be kept, or given to shareholders in the form of dividends.

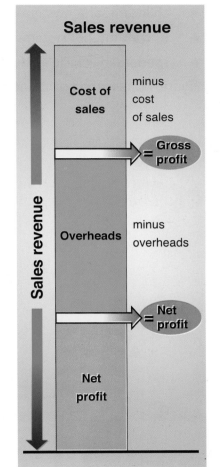

Manchester United uses some of its profits to invest in new players

13 Safety first

Britax

Britax

Britax manufactures equipment for the car and aircraft industries. It produces:

◆ rear vision systems (such as wing mirrors)

◆ childcare safety systems (such as seats with seat belts)

◆ aircraft interior systems (such as seating and seat belts)

◆ specialised vehicle systems (e.g. light bars for police service vehicles).

Figure 1 shows the profit and loss account for Britax in 1998.

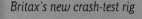
Britax's new crash-test rig

Figure 1 Profit and loss, year ended 31 December 1998

	£000
Sales revenue	621,019
Less Cost of sales	488,873
Gross profit	132,146
Less Overheads	75,024
Net profit	57,122

Source: Annual Report and Accounts, 1998

IN TRAY

1 Is the net profit for Britax higher or lower than it is for Manchester United?

2 What other differences can you see in the profit and loss account?

3 What reasons can you give for the differences?

As a major manufacturer, Britax has to pay for many inputs that would not be needed by businesses in the service sector. It requires a great deal of capital equipment – factories and machinery – and it also has a large budget for **research and development**. Research means using scientific knowledge to find

new and better products and new and better ways to produce them. Development is the process of investigating the best way to do these things.

New **technologies** are very important in helping businesses to make the best products, and they can also help to cut costs. Sometimes that means prices can be cut and more people will buy the product.

Britax products need to be very reliable in use and as safe as possible. The business is constantly trying out new products and improvements and must test everything with the greatest care to ensure that they will be safe.

ACTION

Think of three other businesses that need to spend money on research and development. Explain how this spending will affect profits in the future.

Getting better all the time

Britax takes research and development very seriously. Its products can be steadily improved by using the most modern technology. In order to compete with the best products from all over the world, Britax needs to spend money on its research programme.

One interesting new product is the 'Eyewitness' system of in-car video surveillance. This is now thought to be essential equipment for police cars in the USA.

The 'Eyewitness' in-car video surveillance system

All businesses that make components for motor vehicles face very strong competition. Unless the products are of high quality and reasonably priced, they will not sell.

Many people still want to travel more by air, so there is a growing market for aircraft. But there is also a need to improve the safety of aircraft equipment.

In fact, Britax needs to get better all the time just to stay in business.

IN TRAY

1   Why is quality important?
2   Why does Britax have to keep prices as low as possible?
3   How does research help the business with this?

Figure 2 shows two of the items included in the cost of sales for Britax. In addition, in 1998 the company decided to spend some of its operating profit on new equipment. The amount was £22,100,000.

Figure 2 Cost of sales at Britax

	£000
Capital equipment	19,896
Research and development	16,394

KEY TERMS

⊙—₃₃ **Research and development** make it possible for the business to improve its products and also to find new ones. It may also find new and better ways of producing.

⊙—₃₃ **Technology** is about how products are created. New technologies use science to find better ways of creating products.

CHECKPOINT

1   Altogether, how much did Britax spend on capital equipment?
2   Explain the advantages which research and development can give Britax.

14 Bigger still

Unilever

Unilever is a very large company based partly in the UK and partly in the Netherlands. Because it owns businesses in 68 countries, it is known as a **multinational company**.

Unilever is the parent company of some well-known businesses. You may have come across these:

◆ Birds Eye Wall's Ltd makes food products

◆ Elizabeth Arden Ltd makes cosmetics

◆ Lipton Ltd packages tea

◆ Lever Brothers Ltd makes laundry and cleaning products such as Jif.

Probably almost everyone in the UK uses some of Unilever's products regularly. Unilever's sales revenue was £27 billion in 1998 – that's 43 times as big as Britax's sales revenue and 300 times as big as Manchester United's.

Unilever adds up all the sales revenue for all the companies it owns. It doesn't bother with cost of sales, gross profit and overheads. Its profit and loss account goes straight from sales revenue to net profit. Accounts are like this; the way they are set out can vary from one business to another.

Like most companies, Unilever gives the figures for the last year as well.

Figure 1 Unilever's profit and loss account, 1998 (£ million)

	1998	1997
Sales revenue	27,094	29,776
Net profit	2,955	2,781

ACTION

Take a look at all the cleaning products you can find at home. Most of them will have the name of the maker on the container in very small letters – you will have to look hard. (The brand name is the name in big letters.) Some products may be made by Lever (which is part of Unilever). You may find that there is one other important manufacturer of cleaning products. Which is it? How do this company and Lever compete?

IN TRAY

1 What do you notice about Unilever's profits in 1998 compared to 1997?

2 Now look at the sales revenue for the two years. What do you notice?

3 Suggest reasons why sales revenue and profits changed.

4 Think of another big business you know of which operates in several different countries. What does it sell?

Getting everyone cleaner

Surf is big in the Philippines

Some big multinational businesses have many different products, while others specialise more. They will try to concentrate on the products they find most profitable, which will usually be the ones they are best at producing.

Very profitable businesses can use some of their profits to buy other businesses: there will be a **merger** or a **takeover**. Unilever has done this many times. Ford took over Volvo in 1998.

Where did it all come from?

Unilever explains in its accounts how much of its net profit came from each of its main product groups.

Figure 2 Unilever: net profit (£ million)

	1998	1997
Foods		
Oil and dairy based and bakery	493	535
Ice cream and beverages	399	421
Frozen foods	439	356
Home care	604	537
Personal care	855	856
Other	165	76

And where did it all go to?

Figure 3 Unilever: costs (£ million)

	1998	1997
Wages and saleries	4,065	4,436
Raw materials and packaging	11,860	13,063
Advertising and promotion	3,476	3,628
Reerach and development	556	546
Capital costs	921	1,033
Accountancy	27	20
Administrative expenses	2,577	3,895
Other costs	657	763

IN TRAY

1. Look carefully at Unilever's revenues and costs for 1997 and 1998 and work out some of the reasons for the changes in net profit. Look back at the reasons you suggested earlier. Have the extra figures helped you to understand?

2. Using this information, try to work out what Unilever's main objectives are.

KEY TERMS

☞ A **multinational company** is one that owns businesses in many countries.

☞ A **merger** happens when two big companies combine into one.

☞ A **takeover** happens when a big company buys a smaller one.

15 Let it Snow

OBJECTIVES

To explore the benefits to a company of being able to produce a profit and loss statement on a computer.

How much profit?

Ben, Charlotte, Stephen, Graham and Donovan set up a company as part of their GNVQ business course. They called themselves Let it Snow. During a brainstorming session, the group identified the product that they hoped would sell in the school's Christmas fair – Christmas cards. With the cartoon designs they had in mind, they were sure they'd have plenty of buyers. They would be able to sell the cards at other times as well.

Charlotte had a contact in the school who was a talented designer. Let it Snow would be able to subcontract the design and production of the cards to her. The design would cost £20.00. The production of the cards was an

ACTION

Using Let it Snow's figures, produce your own version of its profit and loss statement using a suitable software package. How long did it take you to produce the spreadsheet? How does this compare with writing out different sets of figures by hand?

Most companies make use of computers to produce their financial statements. The computer can make calculations much faster than a person performing the same task by hand. With a **spreadsheet**, any changes to the figures can be keyed in, allowing financial information to be updated quickly and accurately.

Sell more

Graham opened up Excel on his user area and started to set out the profit and loss statement. You can see this in Figure 1. He assumed that one batch of cards would be produced and that they would all be sold. The design was an overhead cost. Once it was done, they could use it for as many cards as they could sell. Selling costs would also be an overhead. They covered the cost of making and displaying the posters to advertise the cards.

PORTFOLIO PROMPTS

Find out from a business you are studying how it produces its accounts. Find out which system the company uses and why this one was chosen.

Profit and loss for Let it snow, 31st December 1999	
	£
Sales revenue	50
Cost of sales	17
Gross profit	33
Expenses	
Selling costs	10
Design	20
Net profit	3

Figure 1

additional £10.00 for a batch of 50 packs. Each pack would contain six cards.

They decided to start by making one batch of 50 packs. They had to buy envelopes at £1.25 for a pack of 25. They worked out that they would need to pay someone £4.50 for packaging the envelopes together with the cards. The market research they had done showed that Let it Snow would be able to sell the packs at £1.00 each.

Graham, the Financial Director, was given the task of producing a profit and loss statement for the group. 'The problem is,' said Stephen, 'what if sales go up more than we expect? What is our profit then? Do we really want Graham to write everything out by hand every time our sales change?'

Donovan made a suggestion. 'Why can't we do it on the computer? If we use Excel we can change the sales figures and see how the profit changes. The headings are easy enough, and we shouldn't have a problem with the formulae.'

 IN TRAY

1 What are the advantages of putting a profit and loss statement on a spreadsheet?

2 Small businesses need to think carefully about how they will transfer their accounts to a computer. What costs will they need to consider?

The snag was the net profit. Graham was disappointed, as he thought they would make more than that. Then he used his spreadsheet to key in different levels of sales and cost of sales. If they could sell two batches, the profits would improve. You can see what he did in Figure 2.

The formulae he used are shown in Figure 3. Once he had set up the spreadsheet like this the gross and net profit would be calculated automatically. Graham had only to key in the new sales revenue and cost of sales figures.

 **IN TRAY**

1 Why did the profits improve so much if the team could sell two batches of cards?

2 What would happen if the team did not manage to sell all of the second batch of cards?

3 Explain what the formulae in the spreadsheet mean.

Figure 2

Profit and loss for Let it snow, 31st December 1999	
	£
Sales revenue	100
Cost of sales	34
Gross profit	66
Expenses	
Selling costs	10
Design	20
Net profit	36

Figure 3

Profit and loss for Let it snow, 31st December 1999	
	£
Sales revenue	50
Cost of sales	17
Gross profit	= C4 – C6
Expenses	
Selling costs	10
Design	20
Net profit	= C8 – C11 – C12

KEY TERM

A **spreadsheet** is a table set up on a computer using formulae, which automatically update the data as new figures are keyed in.

15a Recording changes

OBJECTIVES

To find out how a new business can grow very big very quickly and understand how this is shown in the accounts.

To consider why a business may make losses.

The future's bright

You may have heard of Orange plc, the mobile phone operator. It's a company in a growing market. In 1999 it made a real net profit for the first time, which pleased the chairman and the directors very much indeed.

By then, 29 per cent of the UK population had a mobile phone. Orange UK expected this figure to rise to 50 per cent by 2001. Orange was getting a larger share of the growth than some other companies.

The Orange vision is for wirefree phones to replace fixed phones. The company expects to find ways to use mobile phones for **data transfer** as well as voice. That means:

◆ Many people will not need a telephone line at home.

◆ People will send emails from their mobiles.

◆ Businesses will send large quantities of data from one computer to another on mobile systems instead of on telephone lines.

This will be important for businesses that gather data from many different places onto one computer system.

Orange UK's good results came from a big increase in the number of subscribers. Also, many subscribers made more calls than before. The profit and loss account shown in Figure 1 compares the first six months of 1999 with the same period in 1998.

Orange plc Interim Report/1999

The future's bright: we continue to build on our strengths with the aim of accelerating delivery of the wirefree future.

Figure I Profit and loss account for Orange UK

	6 months to June 1999	6 months to June 1998
	£ milion	£ million
Sales revenue	813	534
Less cost of sales	597	414
Gross profit	216	120
Less Distribution costs	89	64
Less Administrative expenses	87	54
Net profit	40	2

Source: Annual Report and Accounts

IN TRAY

1 How was it possible for net profit to increase so much in a short time?

2 Why was Orange UK really very pleased with its growth?

3 How has the mobile phone market changed since this was written?

A company that is getting started in a new market has to spend large sums of money, and it may be quite a while before it begins to make a profit. Orange needed a network of masts to transmit the phone messages in a reliable way. It needed to put a lot of money into capital equipment.

Some businesses start very small indeed and grow from nothing. Other businesses have to start fairly large because there is no other way to operate. If they need a great deal of equipment just to have a product, they need support from banks as well as shareholders.

Orange borrowed

To improve its network, Orange had to borrow. In 1999, it had borrowed an extra £259 million. Altogether it had borrowed £1,893 million – that is nearly £2 billion. This staggering debt was costly. Look at the figures for interest payments shown in Figure 2.

Figure 2 The effect of interest payments on Orange UK's net profit

	6 months to June 1999	6 months to June 1998
	£ milion	£ million
Net profit	40	2
Less interest payments	57	51
Loss	− 17	− 49

Orange's net profit was wiped out by the interest it had to pay on the debt.

IN TRAY

1　Why was Orange pleased with a loss of £17 million in 1999?

2　What do you think happened to Orange next?

Man's best friend – a dog or a mobile?

ACTION

See if you can find out what has happened to Orange since 1999. Are its adverts still different? How does it compare with other mobile phone operators? Has the business continued to grow?

KEY TERM

Data transfer means sending large amounts of business or other information by telephone from one computer to another.

15b Who did best?

OBJECTIVES

To construct a profit and loss account from information about the company.

To compare the sales revenue and the net profit of two big supermarket chains.

Sainsbury's

Supermarket chains have grown and have become very powerful. They do compete with each other, however, and shareholders watch their performance with interest.

In 1999, Sainsbury's had sales revenue of £16,433 million (excluding **VAT**). This compared with £14,500 million the previous year. This looks quite good.

Supermarkets have high cost of sales figures as they have to buy huge quantities of products to sell. For Sainsbury's in 1999, cost of sales was £15,095 million, while overheads were £436 million.

IN TRAY

1. Find the percentage growth of Sainsbury's sales revenue from 1998 to 1999.

2. Make out a profit and loss account for Sainsbury's for 1999. Do it on paper.

3. Net profit in 1998 was £762 million. How does the 1999 figure compare with this?

4. How would you say Sainsbury's performed in 1999?

You can use profit and loss figures to judge performance, but unless you know something about the business you may find it quite difficult. Sometimes sales revenue rises because the business has opened more outlets or more supermarkets.

During the year, Sainsbury's opened 18 new supermarkets and ten new Homebase stores. These stores should have added to its sales revenue.

One way to think about performance is to compare the figures with those for another similar business. You may be able to build up a picture by thinking about the two businesses from several different points of view.

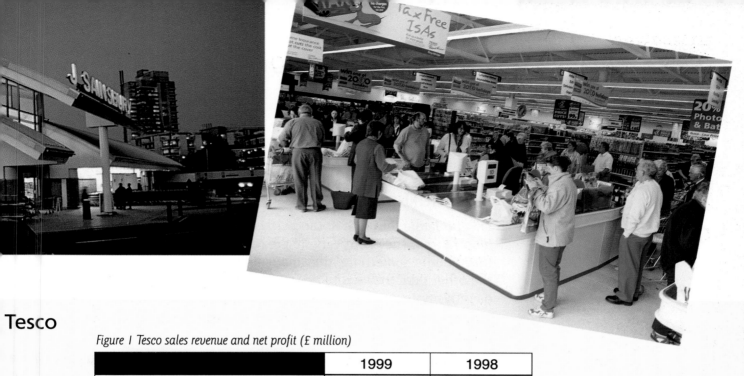

Tesco

Figure 1 Tesco sales revenue and net profit (£ million)

	1999	1998
Sales revenue excluding VAT	17,158	16,452
Expenses	16,224	15,603

Tesco has lumped together its cost of sales and its overheads in one figure for expenses.

IN TRAY

1. Calculate the percentage growth of sales revenue for Tesco.
2. Calculate net profit for Tesco in 1998 and 1999.
3. Did Tesco perform well?
4. How did Tesco's performance compare with Sainsbury's?

ACTION

Visit two different supermarkets and make a note of the following:

◆ the prices of five products in each supermarket

◆ any special features which one has and the other does not

◆ any particular advantages you can see in either supermarket.

When you have done this, try to answer this question: how are these supermarkets competing with each other? Make a list of the ways in which they compete and discuss your findings with other members of the class. Did you all think the same? If you disagreed, say why.

Many people said in 1999 that Tesco was performing better than Sainsbury's. Have you found out anything that supports this view?

Write a short report on all of your findings.

KEY TERM

VAT – Value Added Tax – is a sales tax which is added to the price of the product. It is charged on household products, adult clothes and many other products, but not on food or books.

16 Keep it accurate

Jaz and Jamie's sandwich shop

Jaz and Jamie set up their sandwich shop about 12 months ago. They kept very simple records in a small notebook. Whenever they bought something, they made an entry on one side of the page. On the other side, they wrote down the amount of money they made each day. This system worked well for a year. Then two things happened.

First, they recruited a full-time employee. So far, they had bought the food they needed early in the morning from the markets using cash paid to them the day before. Then they worked together in the shop all day. There was very little time to do paperwork, which had piled up over the year. Their new recruit was going to look after the administration side of their growing business.

Second, their accountant had asked them for their books and records in order to do the first year's accounts. They had a huge pile of receipts, a cheque book and a bank paying-in book. That was all. They hoped their new employee would help to put the information together for the accountant.

OBJECTIVES

To find out why a small business needs to keep accurate records and know how to keep a check on them.

IN TRAY

1 Why is it important for a business to keep proper records of what it spends and what it buys?

2 Why do Jaz and Jamie need an accountant?

3 What might go wrong if cash is used to pay for the inputs?

Businesses must keep accurate records. They need reliable figures to show how much money they are taking from customers. This is known as turnover.

The business also needs to know how much money it is spending. This is known as **expenditure**. The difference between turnover and expenditure shows whether the business is making a profit or a loss. It is also important for the owner of the business to know how much money there is in the bank.

Most businesses have systems that help to keep these records. Sometimes these are manual and the

PORTFOLIO PROMPTS

Find out what arrangements are made to keep accurate records in a business you are studying.

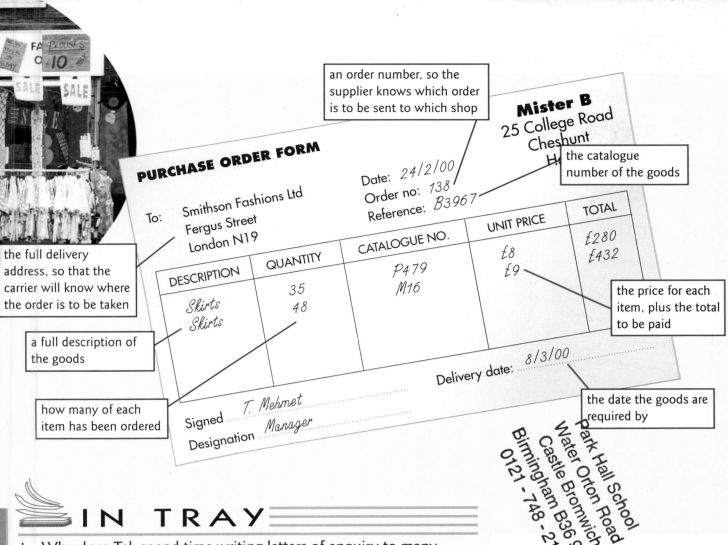

an order number, so the supplier knows which order is to be sent to which shop

the catalogue number of the goods

Mister B
25 College Road
Cheshunt
H.

PURCHASE ORDER FORM

Date: 24/2/00
Order no: 138
Reference: B3967

To: Smithson Fashions Ltd
Fergus Street
London N19

DESCRIPTION	QUANTITY	CATALOGUE NO.	UNIT PRICE	TOTAL
Skirts	35	P479	£8	£280
Skirts	48	M16	£9	£432

Delivery date: 8/3/00

Signed T. Mehmet
Designation Manager

the full delivery address, so that the carrier will know where the order is to be taken

a full description of the goods

how many of each item has been ordered

the price for each item, plus the total to be paid

the date the goods are required by

Park Hall School
Water Orton Road
Castle Bromwich
Birmingham B36 9HF
0121 - 748 - 212

IN TRAY

1 Why does Tek spend time writing letters of enquiry to many different suppliers?

2 How will Tek choose which suppliers he will order from?

3 Make a list of all the details needed on the purchase order.

4 Draw a flow diagram to show all the stages of the order process to make sure the clothes have arrived at the shop.

In some organisations, a **goods received note** may be used, which is completed by the person who receives the delivery. It is a careful check on the goods, making sure that what was actually delivered is the same as what is written on the delivery note.

GOODS RECEIVED NOTE

Mister B
25 College Road
Cheshunt
Herts

Date: 24/2/00
Reference: B3967

To: Smithson Fashions Ltd
Fergus Street
London N19

ORDER NO.	QUANTITY	DESCRIPTION	REF.NO.
138	35	Skirts	P479
	48	Skirts	M16

Received by Tek Mehmet

19 Paying

The goods have arrived

Tek Mehmet often goes to the warehouse himself to collect the clothes he is buying. He checks that everything he ordered is there. There is an **invoice** attached to the clothes he has ordered which tells him when he must pay for them and how much.

Most of the information that was on the order form will be on the invoice.

INVOICE

To:
Mister B
25 College Road
Cheshunt
Herts

Delivery address:
Mister B
25 College Road
Cheshunt
Herts

Smithson Fashions Ltd
Fergus Street
London N19

Order No.: **138**
Invoice No.: **1235**
Despatch date: **8.3.99**

QUANTITY	DESCRIPTION	UNIT PRICE	TOTAL
35	SKIRTS	£8	£280
48	SKIRTS	£9	£432
		Goods total	£712
		INVOICE TOTAL	£712

Terms of payment: 28 days

Tek likes to pay all his bills straight away.
From the seller's point of view, that makes him a good customer. They may even give him better discounts sometimes because he is reliable.

If he is buying from suppliers further away, the invoice comes with the delivery. Within a day or two, Tek will send a **cheque** to settle the debt. A bigger business might have an accounts department which would handle the administration. Tek takes care of all this himself.

IN TRAY

1 What is the purpose of an invoice?

2 Use the information on the purchase order form that you have already created to make out an invoice for the same goods.

The main purpose of an invoice is to give notice that it is time to pay the bill. As such, it is an important document. It is part of the legal agreement between buyer and seller to exchange the goods for a sum of money.

The invoice is sent from the seller to the buyer to advise how much the buyer has to pay for a particular order of goods. It must state:

- the quantity of goods supplied
- individual prices
- any VAT charged
- the total amount owed.

The invoice will also show:

- the address of the supplier

LADIES FASHIONS **Mister B** FACTORY OUTLET

Add some sunshine to your wardrobe! Come down and check our Mad Summer prices

BLOUSES from £8 **TROUSERS from £7.50** **SKIRTS from £6.50**

B for Best Styles
B for Best prices
B for Best value
B for Big sizes

Support your local shops

25 COLLEGE ROAD, CHESHUNT, HERTS EN8 9LS
TEL 01992 63898
Opposite Post Office – Open Monday to Saturday, 9am to 5.30pm
(early closing Wednesday)

- where the invoice should be sent
- where the goods were sent
- carriage paid (if included), which means the price paid includes the delivery of the goods.

Invoices must be dated. If there are any special payment terms, these will be shown. With well-known customers the invoice may say 'net monthly', which means that payment is due within one month.

The individual invoice number and the buyer's order number will both be shown. This enables the buyer to match the invoice with the original purchase order, which will be helpful when checking to see that no mistakes have been made.

Mistakes are costly and it takes time to put them right. Often, this time could be spent doing other things to promote the business. Cutting down on mistakes can mean that administration costs fall.

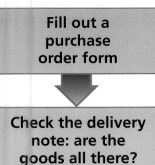

Fill out a purchase order form

↓

Check the delivery note: are the goods all there?

↓

Is the invoice correct for goods actually received?

↓

Has the cheque been sent in payment?

↓

Is the receipt for the right amount?

20 Putting things right

OBJECTIVES

To investigate the purpose of receipts and credit notes.

These aren't the ones

Tek went to the warehouse to collect his next order of clothes. He took a quick look at them and everything seemed to be correct, so he made out a cheque. The warehouse clerk wrote on his invoice, 'paid with thanks', together with the date and his signature. This was his **receipt**: it stated clearly that Tek had paid.

When he got back to the shop, Tek checked the purchase order and found that the clothes were actually a little different from the ones he had ordered. He returned to the warehouse, taking his receipt with him, and asked the clerk to replace the clothes with the right ones. Of course, they had run out of the ones Tek wanted.

Tek was not happy. This was the second time a mistake had been made. Did he really need to use these suppliers? They offered him a **credit note**, which would take the amount he had paid off the invoice for his next order. He decided he would prefer a refund. His cheque was already on its way to the bank, so the warehouse manager gave him a cheque for the value of the clothes. He never went back.

Credit Note

CHEFFIN'S WAREHOUSE SUPPLIES, Queen Street, Watford WD3 2LH

To: Mister B
25 College Road
Cheshunt, Herts

Credit note: CN2021   **Invoice No.:** M327   **Date:** 18/3/2000

QUANTITY	DESCRIPTION	UNIT PRICE	PRICE
26	Jackets	£45	£1170
44	Shirts	£18	£795
		TOTAL PRICE	£1962

IN TRAY

1 Why was it important that Tek had his receipt when he went back to the warehouse?

2 Why should you keep receipts for products you have bought?

Receipts are the customer's proof that they have paid for the product. The seller is legally responsible for making sure that the product is not faulty. The legal term is 'of merchantable quality', meaning that the product should be exactly what the seller says it is. If not, the customer can return it to the shop with the receipt and is entitled to a refund.

Receipts come in many different forms. They all show the name of the business that is selling the goods, the date and the amount received. Some show exactly what the customer has bought, others do not. Cash receipts may come from any shop. Credit card receipts are used if payment is by credit card. Some receipts are handwritten.

Credit notes are used when an exchange rather than a refund is agreed between buyer and seller. Sometimes the business uses an invoice with the word 'credit' added.

ACTION

Look for different kinds of receipt. For each one, say what the product was and why that particular type of receipt was used. See if you can include an invoice marked 'received with thanks'. Sometimes garages give them to the customer after a car repair. Try to find one example of a credit note if you can.

Receipts from the retailer

At Mister B, Tek uses the cash register to issue receipts. When a customer pays for the goods chosen, Tek enters the amount into the cash register and the amount is then printed on the till receipt. Of course, he also accepts credit cards. In this case, he gives a credit card receipt in addition to the till receipt.

A customer who found that her jacket was coming apart at the seams brought it back with the receipt. Tek gave her an immediate refund. He knew he could take the jacket back to the warehouse and get a refund from them. It was a nuisance, but the customer was within her rights.

Sometimes Tek allows customers he knows to bring back clothes they have changed their minds about. If all the labels are in place and the garment has clearly not been worn, he will issue a credit note. This allows the customer to choose something up to the same value instead.

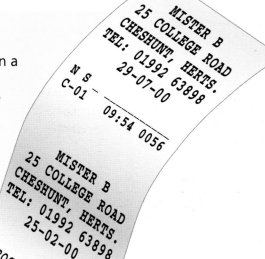

MISTER B
25 COLLEGE ROAD
CHESHUNT, HERTS.
TEL: 01992 63898
29-07-00
N S
C-01
09:54 0056

MISTER B
25 COLLEGE ROAD
CHESHUNT, HERTS.
TEL: 01992 63898
25-02-00
TROSR
BLOUSE   .5.00
CASH   .12.50
C-02   .17.50
16.51 0051

IN TRAY

1 Why did Tek give an immediate refund on the faulty jacket?

2 Why does Tek sometimes allow customers to exchange clothes for a credit note?

KEY TERMS

⊙—ᴛᴛ A **receipt** is a document that shows the amount of money paid for the goods or services.

⊙—ᴛᴛ A **credit note** is a document issued by the supplier which reduces the amount owed by the buyer in the future.

21 Checking

The statement of account for Mister B

Tek's main suppliers send him a **statement of account** every month.

The 'previous balance' is always zero, because Tek pays his bills promptly.

Smithson Fashions Ltd
Fergus Stre
London N

STATEMENT OF ACCOUNT

To:
Mister B
25 College Road
Cheshunt
Herts

Date: 31/3/00
Account No. 286
Reference: B3967

DATE	DETAILS	DEBIT	CREDIT	BALANC
				£0.00
	Previous balance		£0.00	£712
8 March 2000	Goods supplied on Invoice 1235	£712	£0.00	£32
15 March 2000	Goods supplied on Invoice 1309	£326		£1
			AMOUNT DUE	

These are the amounts Tek has to pay for the clothes he bought this month.

IN TRAY

1. What information does the statement of account give?

2. Explain why you think the buyer and the seller need this information.

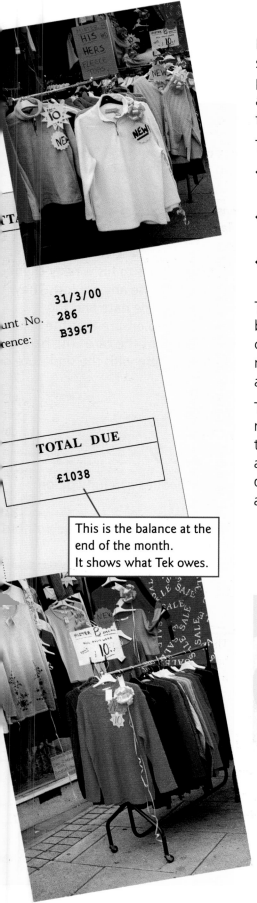

31/3/00

unt No.   286

rence: B3967

TOTAL DUE

£1038

This is the balance at the end of the month.
It shows what Tek owes.

Many businesses settle their accounts with suppliers every month. The suppliers send a statement of account providing details of all the purchases and payments that have taken place. This can be checked against purchase order forms, delivery notes and invoices to see that they all match.

The statement of account will show the following.

◆ Any amounts that have not already been paid, usually shown by the words 'previous balance' or 'balance brought forward'.

◆ Any payments due for goods bought this month which appear in the 'debits' column, with dates.

◆ The amount due at the end of the month, which is at the bottom of the 'balance' column.

The buyer uses the information in order to check that the amounts to be paid are the same as the value of the orders placed. The buyer can check that any previous balance matches the records and that any credit notes have been shown in the credit column. These could reduce the amount to be paid.

The **remittance advice** is a document that shows the total owed. It may be sent to the buyer with the statement of account and is returned to the supplier with the cheque to make payment. The remittance advice gives the account number, date, amount to be paid and invoice details. Some companies attach a tear-off slip to the statement of account, while others use a separate document.

ACTION

Draw a flow chart to describe the way in which all the documents you have studied are used. Show all the important checks that need to be made.

KEY TERMS

🔑 A **statement of account** is a document sent by the seller to the buyer, usually at the end of the month, giving details of invoices, credit notes and any payments made.

🔑 A **remittance advice** is a form sent with the buyer's payment when the invoice or statement of account is settled. It can either be a separate form prepared by the buyer or it can be a tear-off slip sent with the seller's statement.

22 Checks and cheques

Cheques in the shop

Cheques are essential for a business like Mister B. Tek needs to pay his suppliers, and the sums involved are much too big to pay by cash. Also, some of his customers still prefer to pay by cheque.

Like most companies, Mister B only accepts cheques from a customer with a cheque card. This guarantees that the cheque will be paid up to a limit of £50, or sometimes £100.

When a customer pays by cheque, Tek adds the details to his weekly cheque list. His staff keep a careful note of each cheque in case any are lost. They record the bank guarantee card number and check the date and the signature on the cheque and the card. They check to ensure that the value of the cheque does not exceed the guarantee limit of the card. The bank can return any cheques unpaid if there is a problem with the signature or the value of the guarantee.

IN TRAY

1   Why do the staff examine cheques carefully before accepting them?

2   What will happen if someone accepts a cheque without a guarantee card?

Most cheques are handwritten, so care must be taken by both the customer and the seller. These are the things to look out for

Is the payee's name correct? If not, it should be changed and initialled by the customer.

Is the cheque dated correctly? A cheque becomes out of date after six months.

Do the words and figures agree? If not, it may be returned by the bank.

Is the cheque signed? If not, it is not valid.

Date 28-2-00
Payee
Mister B
Old balance
Deposits
Total
This Cheque £ 13-50
New balance

100281

★ ANYBANK
THE BUSINESS CENTRE
P.O. BOX 15
ANYTOWN AN3 4BQ

Pay —— Mister B ——

Thirteen Pounds 50 ——

ACCOUNT PAYEE

Cheque No.
"100281"   Branch No.
20 48 53   Account No.
34568976

20 48 53

Date 28—2—00

£ 13—50

MS K. BYRON

K Byron

If the customer does not have a guarantee card and there is no money in the account, the cheque will bounce. It will be sent back to the seller without being paid into the account. This could mean a loss on the sale and can be serious for the business.

Paying in cheques

Tek takes his cheques to the bank nearly every day. He has a business paying-in book with a **paying-in slip** for the bank and a counterfoil for his records. He records all the cheque details on the paying-in slip so that the bank can pay cheques straight into his account. His account number is printed on the slip.

If he pays in cash – notes and coins – at the same time, he can put them on the same paying-in slip. They will all be sorted and counted carefully.

At the end of the month the bank will send a **statement**, which gives Tek one more chance to check that everything is correct. He will check the credit items against his paying-in slips and the debit items against his own cheque stubs and the invoices he has paid.

ACTION

1 Find out whether your local bank has leaflets that show how it helps its small business customers. Use these to help you to understand what banks can do. Some businesses find that banks help them less than they had hoped. Why might this be?

2 Find out what the bank charges small businesses for making payments and paying in cheques. Are there other ways for businesses to pay their bills?

IN TRAY

1 Explain what the paying-in slip shows.

2 Explain why it is important to check the bank statement carefully.

The paying-in slip shows the following details:

Boxes to record the amounts paid in.

The name of the bank and the branch and the account number and name.

The counterfoil for the customer's records.

A space for the customer to sign.

Bank statements provide a running balance, which shows how much money has been in the account at all times. As well as payments, they record bank charges. Most businesses have to pay for every cheque used and every payment into the account. If there is an overdraft, there will be interest charges as well.

PORTFOLIO PROMPTS

Find out how the bank has helped a business you are studying.

KEY TERMS

☞ A **paying-in slip** is used to identify all the money paid into a particular account.

☞ A **bank statement** lists all the amounts paid into or out of an account.

23 Speedier and safer

Quality Cases Ltd

Quality Cases Ltd is a small packaging company that produces paper-related products for the food, electrical, clothing and engineering industries. At the moment, Quality Cases uses a paper-based document system, which means that all the financial documents are pre-printed and then filled in by hand. The forms are separated by carbon paper so that several copies may be made at the same time. This means that there is always a way of checking each document, as a copy is held in a file.

Unfortunately, mistakes have caused problems. A long-standing customer, Ness Point Foods, has phoned the accounts office to say that there is a problem with an invoice – it is £150 too much. The goods were delivered three weeks ago. There were three pallets of boxes, each pallet containing a thousand boxes. The agreed price was £1,050, but the invoice was for £1,200.

Angie Reynolds, the accounts clerk, looked into the matter. This was not the first mistake, and there had been several complaints over the previous month. She found the purchase order form and saw that the sales office had agreed the price of £1,050 with the customer.

IN TRAY

1 How could such a mistake have been made?

2 What will Quality Cases have to do to put things right?

3 How might these kinds of problems be prevented in the future?

Businesses check financial documents carefully because mistakes take so long to sort out. A mistake with an invoice usually means checking the purchase order form and the delivery note. If the invoice has been paid before the problem is noticed, the seller will have to send a credit note. The next statement of account will have to be carefully revised so that it puts the matter right. The business will want to sort mistakes out quickly. If there are too many problems, the customer may look for another supplier.

Many businesses use a computerised system for their financial documents. Some can use an 'off-the-shelf' package designed for business users generally. Others will need a **bespoke** system, designed just for their business.

The drawback to a computerised system is that the computer can crash. If it is out of order, no work can be done on the documents. It is important that all information is carefully **backed up** so that it cannot be lost.

ACTION

Contact a computer software company and find out what kinds of software are available for small businesses. Find out the prices and what the different systems can do.

Angie sorts it out

Next, Angie looked for the delivery note. She found that all three pallets had been delivered and signed for. Then she realised that the invoice had been made out at the rate charged for every thousand boxes, which was £400. The sales department had agreed a reduced rate of £350 because the customer was taking a larger quantity. She sent out a corrected invoice immediately.

Angie could see that the invoice had been made out from the delivery note, not from the purchase order form. She thought that if the details agreed with the customer had been on computer, there would have been no mistake because the price would have been written on the invoice automatically.

When Derek Alcott, the managing director, heard about the problems, he called a meeting. 'We have continued to use our present system because it has served us well. However, we recognise that the company must move on and invest in more up-to-date systems if we are going to improve our efficiency,' he told everyone.

IN TRAY

1 Why do you think Quality Cases is considering changing to a computer system to produce its financial documents?

2 What advantages do you think the company will gain from investing in a computer system?

KEY TERMS

✏ A **bespoke** system is a computer software package designed for your use only.

✏ **Backing up** means making a copy of the information that has been processed by the computer.

205

24 Bad documents

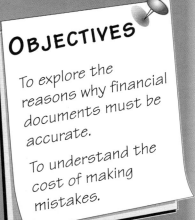

OBJECTIVES

To explore the reasons why financial documents must be accurate.

To understand the cost of making mistakes.

Whoops!

Wendy works in the parts department of Kelly & Sons garage. She orders parts when stocks are running low.

She invoices customers who have had their cars repaired. The mechanic puts the cost on a form and passes it to Wendy, who keys the details into the computer and makes out an invoice. At the end of each month, she sends statements to all those customers who have not paid their invoices straight away.

The trouble is, Wendy is not having a very good day. She missed the bus and came in late. All four telephones were ringing when she arrived. By the time she came to the fourth call, the telephone had been ringing rather a long time. The customer on the other end of the telephone was angry. He had received an invoice for £865.00 for a service on his car. Wendy tried to calm him down and agreed to look into the matter.

INVOICE

Kelly & Sons

23 New Street
Bridgetown
WR3 0HR

To:
Mr Smith
4 Greenwood Terrace
Bridgetown

Invoice No.:
1438

Despatch date:
24 March 2000

Work carried out

£865

Car repairs

INVOICE TOTAL   £865

Terms of payment: 28 days

≡ IN TRAY ≡

1	Make a list of possible reasons why the invoice might have been wrong.
2	Where would you start looking for the problem if you were Wendy?
3	What effect do mistakes like this have?
4	How can they be avoided?

There are two major problems that arise when mistakes are made. One is that mistakes often take some time to sort out. The people who put things right are being paid to do so. Costs can be cut by making fewer mistakes.

The other major problem is that customers are annoyed by mistakes. This is why many businesses make customer service a high priority. If mistakes do happen, they want customers to feel that everything that can be done to help will be done.

Wendy puts it right

A lorry was unloading a large stock of oil. Wendy remembered that the order was quite small, so she was puzzled.

Before she could investigate, she saw a letter on her desk and a note from her boss. The letter was from a supplier. She had sent a cheque for the wrong amount. The supplier had received a cheque for £36,533, but it was still owed £245.99 and payment was two months late. It said it would not supply any more parts until the account was settled. Wendy's boss was not pleased.

Then the delivery man came in with the delivery note. Wendy went outside to check everything. Instead of 100 cans of oil, there were 100 boxes of 20 cans of oil. She tried to talk the delivery man into taking them back. 'It's the paperwork, you see, it will all have to be changed. The delivery note will be wrong, the computer will be wrong – no, sorry, can't do.'

Wendy went back to her office. How could she deal with everything before anyone else got angry?

She looked at the invoice. It should have been for £365.00, not £865.00. She had keyed the wrong amount into her computer. She cancelled the invoice and issued the customer with a credit note and a new invoice. This would appear on the statement the customer received at the end of the month. She hoped he would accept her apology.

The cheque she had sent covered an invoice she had received, but there was an invoice missing. She called the supplier, who found it had made out an invoice for the wrong amount and thrown it away. However, the invoice still appeared on the computer as being owed by Kelly & Son. The supplier agreed to continue to supply the garage with parts.

IN TRAY

1 How would you deal with the problem of the oil delivery?

2 What system could Wendy put in place to avoid keying in the wrong amount when she invoices a customer?

3 Wendy put things right, but there had been a great many mistakes. What action would you suggest to ensure that fewer mistakes are made?

PORTFOLIO PROMPTS

Complete a set of documents for the sale and purchase of a particular product. Explain what will happen if a mistake is made at each stage of the process.

ACTION

Ask someone who is in business to tell you about a mistake that was made not long ago. What was done to put it right?

25 A constant flow of fashion

OBJECTIVES

To find out how a new business manages its cash flow during the time when start-up costs have to be covered and a customer base is developed.

Wild Heart

Heather wanted to start her own fashion boutique. She found that she could rent premises just off the high street. She knew she would have to keep the shop well stocked with clothes in order to attract enough customers.

The fittings for the shop were going to be expensive, but they would make it stylish and attractive. Her only other costs would be heating, lighting, carrier bags, a till, insurance and the telephone. She would have to work hard herself, but she hoped she could soon employ a Saturday helper and a cleaner.

Heather had saved some money to start her dream shop. She had also borrowed some money from her parents and had written a business plan that persuaded her bank manager to lend her the rest.

She had to make sure she could cover her costs every month and keep the shop stocked with clothes that her customers liked. She also had to ensure customers actually came into the shop and bought the clothes.

Heather closed her shop every Wednesday and went to London to buy stock. She always looked for the latest fashion items and would also buy more of items that were selling well. Sometimes a customer would ask her to look out for something special or different. Heather would often buy to suit her regular customers and kept them in mind when she bought her stock.

ACTION

Imagine you are Heather. You have to produce a business plan that will persuade the bank manager to lend you money. What information will need to be included in the plan?

IN TRAY

1   What were Heather's start-up costs?

2   How did Heather finance the business she had started?

3   How was Heather able to buy new stock?

4   How did Heather attract her customers?

In order to generate a flow of cash through any business, there must be a product or a service that will sell to the customer. Prices need to be higher than the cost of buying or making the product, otherwise it will be impossible to cover all the costs. Keeping track of how much is sold and at what cost is very important if the business is going to succeed.

To make sure the business survives, the **cash flow** must be calculated each month. This means adding up all the cash outflow – the costs actually paid during that month. The cash inflow includes all the sales revenue that has come in. The difference between them is the cash flow. (This is sometimes called the net cash flow.)

Bringing in the cash

Heather had the money she had saved and borrowed to buy the stock and open the shop. It was important to make sure the goods sold quickly in order to generate enough cash to allow her to buy more stock the following Wednesday.

Heather needed to keep track of her costs. She had to make sure she paid all her bills before she bought new stock. She also had to work out the cost of selling each garment. She needed to make a profit, but she wanted to sell the clothes at a reasonable price. In this way, she could turn over her stock very quickly. This she knew would encourage her customers to come in and buy more often.

IN TRAY

1　How would Heather check all her cash inflows and outflows?

2　How could Heather avoid becoming short of cash?

PORTFOLIO PROMPTS

For a business you have been studying, make a list of costs that have to be met each month. Will the sales revenue always be enough to cover the costs? In which months is there likely to be a problem? If you are thinking about a mini-enterprise, look at the costs and revenues week by week.

KEY TERMS

Cash flow is all of the cash inflows to the business for, say, a month, minus all the cash outflows. It may sometimes be negative. Cash inflows will usually come from sales revenue, while cash outflows will come from paying the bills that cover the costs.

26 Cash crisis

Making the right choices

Owning a small business can be risky. When Heather started Wild Heart, she knew she would need to buy wisely and sell at a reasonable price.

If she has too much stock, she will have less money in the bank. She keeps a careful eye on how well the stock is selling and what remains on the rails. Each month she has bills to pay, which must be paid whether she has sold anything or not. She also now pays a cleaner and two Saturday staff.

She needs money in the bank to buy new stock even if she has not sold all the stock she has already bought. Mostly she is good at what she does, but once she bought a whole batch of trousers, thinking they would be very popular. She sold hardly any. She had tied money up in something that didn't sell.

In order to buy more stock and pay all her monthly bills, she had to ask the bank to lend her some more money for a short period of time. This kind of borrowing is known as an overdraft.

IN TRAY

1 What was the consequence of Heather's buying stock that didn't sell?

2 What costs does Heather have to pay every month, however much or little she sells?

3 Why is making the right choice so important when Heather is buying for her shop?

In business, there are always times when more cash is coming in and times when there is less. Buying stock or the materials to make a product can often mean spending large sums of money and then having to wait for sales revenue until the customer has bought the goods.

In order to be able to pay all the running costs of the business, the owners will negotiate with their bank a short-term loan known as an overdraft. The bank knows that as the business generates revenue it will replace the money borrowed. Of course the bank charges interest, which can itself add to costs.

Later ...

Heather was very successful. She had a good eye for the right clothes and her reputation grew. She began to attract customers from neighbouring towns.

She started to sell accessories such as watches and handbags. She also started to sell larger items such as coats and jackets, which took longer to sell because they were more expensive. It was good to have them in the shop because sometimes people who bought a handbag or a watch would also buy some clothes.

As Heather's business grew she developed good relationships with the companies from which she bought her stock. Her favourite suppliers had imaginative clothes and something different to offer. Some of them offered her **trade credit**, which meant she wouldn't have to pay for her stock for six weeks. This had an impact on her cash flow, as she was able to sell the clothes before she had to pay for them.

IN TRAY

1 Why wasn't Heather able to sell larger and more expensive items when she first started?

2 How would adding coats to her range affect Heather's cash flow?

3 How would the trade credit affect her cash flow?

A business will often sell goods to a customer giving them time to pay. The customer will place an order and take delivery of the goods. They will receive an invoice, which will tell them how much the goods will cost and when they will have to pay for them. The amount of time they are given may be seven days, one month, or even three months if the customer has a very good relationship with the suppliers.

ACTION

1 Find out from the school office what kind of credit terms suppliers give for school supplies.

2 Compare two high street clothes shops, perhaps one that is a chain store and one that is individually owned like Heather's shop. Make observations about their level of stock, the way it is displayed and whether there are sale items. Are there any differences between the two?

KEY TERM

Trade credit is given by manufacturers and wholesalers and allows buyers to get some sales revenue before they have to pay the bill.

211

27 It's a man's world

SQWEAR

Sqwear

Richard and Steve were considering opening a boutique selling clothes for men. They had seen the formula used to make Wild Heart a success and thought they could re-create it. Their shop would be in Stafford. Apart from high street chains, there was very little competition.

They went to see their bank manager for advice. Richard had some money, but he knew from talking to other boutique owners that he would need help at times in the year when cash flow would be low. They would also need some help to get started.

The bank manager insisted that they make a business plan setting out exactly what they would do. She said it must include a 12-month **cash-flow forecast**, showing the peaks and troughs that might occur during the first year of trading.

Figure 1 The first two months: overhead cost

Cash flow	September	October
Rent	1000	1000
Rates	750	750
Electricity	300	
Telephone		100
Wages	188	188
Salary	1400	1400
Bank loan	560	560
Overheads	4198	3998

Richard and Steve opened a spreadsheet on their computer at home and worked out the month-by-month running costs, which included rent and rates. They were able to use figures suggested by the bank to work out the cost of electricity, telephone, insurance and wages. Working out these fixed costs was the easy part.

IN TRAY

1   Why is accurate forecasting important for a business?

2   Would the costs shown in the spreadsheet be about the same each month?

3   What might change?

A cash-flow forecast is simply an estimate that shows how much money will possibly be needed to make the business viable in the first 12 months. A bank will insist on seeing a document like this before it will ever agree to back a small business that is just setting up.

The first task when putting together a cash-flow forecast is to estimate all the costs of the business. These may be much higher in some months than they are in others. Overheads may be fairly steady, but the cost of other inputs may vary.

Deciding when to buy

Richard and Steve found estimating the cost of buying stock difficult. They planned to open the business in September, taking advantage of the Christmas trade. They would buy their first stock just before opening, and then buy small amounts of stock in October and more in November. They knew they would have no time in December. They would restock in February and March for spring and summer, and then buy small amounts of stock from April to June. They would be unlikely to buy much in July, when they would concentrate on their summer sale.

Figure 2 The first 12 months: stock costs

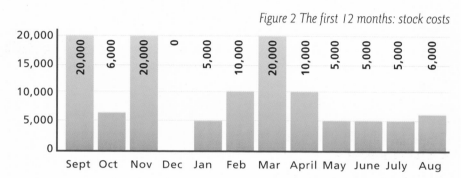

Next, Richard and Steve had to estimate monthly sales. They thought September would be a good month: people would come into the shop out of interest and perhaps buy on impulse. October and November were traditionally good months for selling clothes, and December was usually good for selling anything. January was often a poor month because people had no money left for luxury items. During this month, though, they would

Figure 3 The first 12 months: sales

have a sale to make room for new stock for the spring. This would help boost sales a little. February is always a difficult time to sell clothes, but there is a lot of activity with buying new stock for spring and summer.

IN TRAY

1   In which months would costs be at their highest and lowest?

2   Some businesses have seasonal changes. Explain how these would be likely to affect Sqwear.

ACTION

Using a spreadsheet, construct a cash-flow forecast of your own income and outgoings. Include all the ways in which you receive money and all the different items on which you spend money. Estimate the figures for the next six months.

KEY TERM

⊙━╖ A **cash-flow forecast** shows all the costs and the sales revenue each month over a period of a year. Total cash outflow and inflows are calculated.

28 Picturing the numbers

Forecasting the future

Having worked out their overheads and the cost of stock each month, and their likely sales, Richard and Steve were ready to forecast their cash flow. They had to start by finding the opening balance.

Richard had £12,000 of his own savings to put into the business. He and Steve thought they needed start-up capital of £20,000 altogether, so they would need to ask the bank for a loan of £8,000. You can see this money in the opening balance at the beginning of September in their cash-flow forecast.

Part of Richard and Steve's spreadsheet showing their cash flow for the first five months of trading can be seen in Figure 1. The sales figures show the cash inflow. The cash outflow shows the total spent on all overhead costs, together with the cost of all the clothes they bought for the shop.

Figure 1 The first five months: cash flow

Sqwear					
	September	October	November	December	January
Overheads	4,198	3,998	3,898	4,358	3,998
Stock	20,000	6,000	20,000	0	5,000
Cash outflow	24,198	9,998	23,898	4,358	8,998
Sales	12,000	15,000	18,000	20,000	12,500
Cash flow	-12,198	5,002	-5,898	15,642	3,502
Opening balance	20,000	7,802	12,804	6,906	22,548
Closing balance	7,802	12,804	6,906	22,548	26,050

ACTION

Ask your local bank for a copy of the cash-flow forms it gives to possible new businesses. Think of a business that you might want to start up. Using the paperwork from the bank, fill in what you would expect to spend on fixed costs (overheads). Then work out all the other costs, and the revenue, for each of the 12 months. Use a spreadsheet to calculate the opening and closing balances. Show below your spreadsheet the formulae you have used.

IN TRAY

1 Which are the best and the worst months for cash flow between September and January?

2 Do you think the big variations in sales are going to be a problem?

3 What could happen that might make these forecasts inaccurate?

4 Does Sqwear always have a closing balance large enough to pay for the next month's stocks?

In addition to the estimates of costs and sales revenue, the cash-flow forecast must show the **start-up capital**. This is the amount of money that can be put into opening the business. It comes from the owners' savings and any bank loans they can get. This will be the **opening balance**. The cash flow for the month, added to the opening balance, gives the **closing balance** at the end of the month. This becomes the opening balance for the next month.

Once the business is up and running, it is a good idea to monitor how it is actually doing against the forecast made. In this way, cash flow can be measured and stock levels checked.

Sometimes the business may not be generating very much sales revenue, so that the flow of cash will be negative. At other times, when the business is doing well, perhaps at Christmas, there will be a positive flow of cash into the business.

If the owner of the business is able to predict these fluctuations, it is much easier to convince a bank manager to help out when cash is scarce and an overdraft is needed. If the cash flow is negative, the closing balance may go below zero. Then swift action is needed to make sure the bank will help with an overdraft.

Making a cash-flow forecast

Work out all the overheads.

Add the costs of all other inputs.

Calculate monthly cash outflow.

Calculate sales revenue (inflow) minus cash outflow to arrive at cash flow.

Find opening balance for first month.

Add cash flow to opening balance to arrive at closing balance.

The closing balance becomes next month's opening balance.

PORTFOLIO PROMPTS

Using a business you have studied, explain what happens each month of the year to costs and revenue within the business. Explain how cash flow will be affected.

KEY TERMS

○⊐ **Start-up capital** is the money the business has to finance its opening and early months.

○⊐ The **opening balance** in a cash-flow forecast is the amount of cash in the bank at the beginning of the month.

○⊐ The **closing balance** in a cash-flow forecast is the amount of cash in the bank at the end of the month.

29 An uneven year

OBJECTIVES

To explore how seasonal variations affect the cash flow of a business, and how a business might try to offset them.

Coalport youth hostel

Adrian and Sally Dye run Coalport youth hostel near the industrial heritage town of Ironbridge in Shropshire. Ironbridge has nine museums and is surrounded by beautiful countryside.

The youth hostel was originally part of the Coalport china factory. It has been refurbished and its brick and iron interior is light, spacious and very comfortable.

Adrian and Sally run the hostel as a business. They carefully control their costs and constantly market their services. Visitors come mainly in the summer when the museums are busy. Schools visit in the spring and autumn. This means they are very quiet in the winter. They try to use their quiet period wisely by carrying out maintenance and cleaning, but they would really prefer to have more visitors.

The Coalport hostel has a café that is open to the public. This is why the youth hostel remains open all year round.

IN TRAY

1 Why is it important for Adrian and Sally to plan ahead for very busy or very quiet times?

2 What costs will they have to cover in the winter?

3 How will costs change in the summer?

4 Work out how these changes affect their cash flow.

In every business the costs and the sales revenue generated will fluctuate from month to month. Some businesses are more seasonal than others. A business that sells coal will obviously be busier in the winter than in the summer. A business that runs a caravan park on the Devon coast will be busier in the summer than in the winter. Every business has to plan for its busy and quiet periods. It must make sure it has enough stock to sell when there is a high demand, while stocks should be kept lower during quiet times.

If the cash flow is going to be negative in some months, the business must work out ways to cover its costs. Sales revenue may be sufficient in earlier months to cover the difference in quiet months.

The YHA mission statement

'To help all, especially young people of limited means, to a greater knowledge, love and care of the environment.'

The Youth Hostel Association (YHA) has 230 hostels and houses in the United Kingdom, with 13,711 bed spaces available per night. There are youth hostels in most major cities and rural locations. Each one has its own individual character, attracting different sorts of people. The YHA is a charity. If one hostel does not make a profit, it may still be kept open if it benefits the community.

Ilam Hall

Bev and Sue Bamber work very hard to make the youth hostel they manage at Ilam Hall in Derbyshire busy all year round. They have two very different trades.

In May, June and July they have a great many young school parties, combining an educational visit with outdoor pursuits. They have a very busy summer with families who like to walk in the surrounding Peak District. In the autumn they are busy again with schools, although this time the groups are usually older students on field study trips.

Bev and Sue are trying to market their business through the winter to offset the drop in their cash flow and to make sure their magnificent premises are not under-used. They have created a winter trade with conferences and training days, which has reduced their negative cash flow in the winter.

CHECKPOINT

1 How does the Youth Hostel Association generate revenue?

2 List some of the costs of running the YHA.

3 Will there be times when cash flow is very low?

PORTFOLIO PROMPTS

Find out how cash flow is affected by seasonal variations in a business you have studied. Is anything done to try to increase sales during the quieter months?

IN TRAY

1 How will cash flow be affected by the seasonal pattern of sales revenue?

2 What difference will the winter trade in conferences make to cash flow?

30 Watching the inputs

OBJECTIVES

To find out how a manufacturing business controls its cash flow.

Perkins Engines Ltd

Perkins makes diesel engines for use in trains, tanks and hospital generators. A very important objective for this business is to deliver the product on time and made exactly to the customer's specification.

Perkins has to make sure that supplies of all inputs are available in the right quantity at exactly the right time. There must be enough skilled people available to work on the production lines and enough money to pay everyone. That means the cash must be flowing.

The management watches stocks of inputs very carefully. Paying for stocks that are not needed is not very sound business practice. Stored components take up valuable space, and someone must look after the storage area.

Perkins operates a system called just-in-time (JIT). It buys just the amount of stock needed to satisfy the orders it has from customers and does not keep extra stocks of inputs. This means it is not tying up its cash in goods that might not be used for some time.

IN TRAY

1   Explain what is meant by just-in-time.

2   How can just-in-time stock control help the cash flow?

3   What would happen if Perkins ran out of the inputs it needs to make up an urgent order?

ACTION

Find out how often your school orders supplies of paper and exercise books. Why might people in schools keep stocks for quite a long period?

Every business has to be sure that it has enough **working capital**. In other words, there must be cash in the bank so that it can pay for all its essential inputs. In a manufacturing business, this is very important.

Just-in-time stock-keeping can help to cut the cost of keeping stocks and reduces the cash outflow. However, it means that the business must have a very good relationship with its suppliers. Managers must be sure that they can rely on their suppliers to deliver everything promptly. They also need to be sure that the goods are in perfect condition and will not have to be sent back. If the supplier lets them down, they will have to let their customer down by being late with the delivery of their order.

Less cash

Perkins is very careful about cash flow and has built up good relationships with its suppliers. Racks of nuts and bolts supplied by a nut and bolt manufacturer are placed along the production line. Perkins does not pay for them until they have been used in the production process. Every few weeks, the racks are refilled and only the number used is charged for. Perkins is not tying up cash in buying more of these items than it needs.

The buyers at Perkins work closely with suppliers to try to secure the best possible payment terms. They want to have the supplies in order to make the engines, but they do not want to pay for those supplies straight away. If they can get trade credit they will have less cash tied up in the manufacturing process.

The engine cases are stored at the Perkins factory because it has more space than the case manufacturer. Perkins only pays for the cases when they are used. The case manufacturer is happy because storage is expensive, and Perkins is happy because it has an expensive item on site for use at any time.

IN TRAY

1 Why is it important for Perkins to have a good relationship with suppliers?

2 Explain how good relationships with suppliers can reduce the cash outflow.

The more it can keep cash outflows down, the less working capital the business needs. That means less borrowing, less interest to pay and more profit.

Cost of stocks kept down with JIT	$\Rightarrow$	Less cash needed for storage	$\Rightarrow$	Less borrowing	$\Rightarrow$	Less interest to pay	$\Rightarrow$	More profit

PORTFOLIO PROMPTS

Find out how often deliveries are made to a local retailer that you have studied. How long does it expect its stocks to last?

KEY TERMS

Working capital is cash which the business needs to cover its costs up to the time when the products are delivered and paid for.

31 It all went wrong

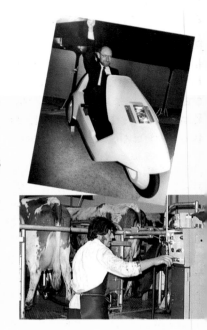

OBJECTIVES

To investigate why things sometimes go wrong in business and how this affects cash flow.

Anyone can make a mistake

◆ Clive Sinclair's C5 electric car was predicted to be a great success but was in fact a dramatic failure.

◆ BSE in cattle damaged the farming industry very badly and left many small farmers in debt or bankrupt.

◆ Marks & Spencer struggled with poor sales because its range of clothes and underwear was not what its customers wanted to buy.

◆ Perrier, the bottled water company, suffered a blow when a poisonous chemical was found to have contaminated its product.

◆ The estimate to build the Channel Tunnel was £4 billion. In the event, it cost its owners, Eurotunnel, £10 billion.

◆ Next plc closed its operations in the USA and Europe because it was not making any money there.

IN TRAY

1 Explain what happens to costs, sales revenues and cash flow when a product is faulty.

2 What must a business do if it finds that its products are not selling well?

When they construct a cash-flow forecast, people going into business assume they know what will happen. However, events may turn out quite differently.

In manufacturing, the product that comes off the production line must be fit for its purpose. It must be made to a standard that is expected by the customer. If it doesn't work, if it is missing a part or is the wrong size, it will not do and the customer will send it back. The cost of poor quality is enormously high to a manufacturer.

Supplies have been used during the production process. These may now be scrapped or will need to be dismantled and used again. This all takes time. People have been employed to produce the goods, the machinery has been tied up and will need to be used again in order to rework the product. The customer will be dissatisfied because delivery is late. Money has been spent on supplies, using the machinery and paying staff. The unhappy customer will not be paying for faulty or unfit merchandise.

This can't happen too often or the business will soon have very serious cash-flow problems. It will be considered unreliable and its customers will go elsewhere.

Maintaining cash flow in a shop can be difficult, too. The shop must buy the goods the customer wants. Stocks of goods for sale tie up a lot of cash. Stock must turn over quickly so that more can be purchased. If the customer goes into the shop and the stock is the same as last time and the time before, they are unlikely to keep going back and so a customer will be lost.

Stock in a shop needs to be fresh and new, appealing and attractive. Whether the shop sells food, records, clothes, toys or electrical goods, the products need to be what the customer wants. Fashions, trends, new technology all need to be considered in order that the outflows generate inflows and cash flow remains positive.

All businesses will find that cash flow is healthy if they can control quality, avoid mistakes and please the customer.

CHECKPOINT

1 Why is the cost of poor quality in the manufacturing process so high?

2 What do shopkeepers have to consider when they are buying merchandise?

ACTION

1 See if you can add to the list of things that can go wrong in a business. Explain how the things that go wrong affect cash flow.

2 Choose a product that you use regularly. Make a list of what you expect from the product. Make another list of all the things that could have been wrong with it when you bought it.

3 Go into a local shop and take a look at the merchandise for sale. Ask yourself if it is attractive, fashionable, innovative, high-tech, clean or fresh. Compare a successful shop with one that does not seem to do so well.

PORTFOLIO PROMPTS

Explain how mistakes can affect the cash flow of a business you have studied. Give examples of mistakes that have happened or could happen.

32 Costs and cutting

The cost of a haircut

Tracey runs her own men's hairdressing business called TC's. Like anyone running their own business, she is very much aware of the cost of keeping the business going. She has a small salon, which she rents. She charges £5 for a basic haircut, with extras costing more. She is open five days a week, Tuesday to Saturday. The busiest day is Saturday, when she employs another hairdresser to work part-time. Tracey pays herself the same salary each week and her assistant's pay is also the same each week.

OBJECTIVES

To find out what fixed costs are and how they can be represented on a graph.

IN TRAY

1   What costs do you think Tracey has to meet even if she has no customers?

2   What other costs do you think she is likely to have?

The costs that have to be met even if there are no customers are usually referred to as **fixed costs**. These costs are the same, week by week and month by month. Here are some examples of fixed costs.

◆   **Premises**
Small businesses usually have to pay rent for their premises. In addition, all businesses pay business rates to the local authority.

◆   **Insurance**
Most businesses insure their premises and equipment against the risk of a fire or burglary. The insurance premiums might be paid monthly.

◆   **Lighting**
Shops, in particular, keep their lights on all day, regardless of the time of year. This then becomes a fixed cost.

◆   **Loans**
Many businesses have to borrow money, especially when they are being set up. Loans might be for equipment and machinery. Both interest and repayments will be paid back monthly.

PORTFOLIO PROMPTS

Make a list of the fixed costs of the business you are investigating.

◆ Salaries

In many businesses staff are paid a salary for the year and receive the same pay each week or month. These are then fixed costs.

◆ Advertising

Some businesses advertise on a regular basis. Their advertising can be done in many ways. Some businesses set aside a budget for advertising, which can be seen as a cost spread throughout the year.

No matter how many items are produced or services provided for customers, a business has to pay all the fixed costs. They are sometimes called overheads. Fixed costs vary between businesses. A hairdressing business will have very different costs to a car manufacturer.

A manufacturing business will usually have very high costs for factory buildings and machinery. These are fixed costs, too. Even if there is no production because of a breakdown or perhaps because there are too few customers, the costs have to be covered somehow.

These costs can be shown in the form of a graph. This graph shows that no matter what the output of the business, the fixed costs remain the same.

The fixed costs can be grouped together and represented by a single line on the graph.

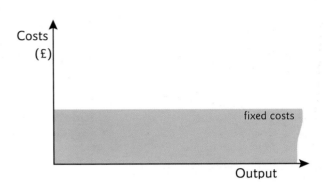

Tracey's costs

The table shows how Tracey's fixed costs work out each week.

Tracy's costs					
No. of haircuts	Rent	Rates	Salaries	Loans	Fixed costs
	£	£	£	£	£
0	50	35	450	40	
20	50	35	450	40	
40	50	35	450	40	
60	50	35	450	40	
80	50	35	450	40	
100	50	35	450	40	
120	50	35	450	40	

IN TRAY

1 Calculate the fixed costs at each level of output.
2 Draw a graph to show Tracey's fixed costs.

33 The costs of making more

What changes?

Aaron is great at making furniture and runs his own business. His rented workshop is a converted stable on a farm, and so he named his business Pine Stable. He makes a range of items out of wood, usually pine, including tables, cupboards, fire surrounds and bookcases. He has a number of standard designs but does make items to customers' specifications. He works on his own, so his output is quite low.

In addition to rent and rates, Aaron has other costs. He uses raw materials, mainly wood. He also uses glue, wax, stain, knobs, hinges and electricity to run the machinery. His friend delivers items for him and is paid for each delivery made.

As Aaron produces more items, he uses more wood, wax, hinges and so on. He will therefore spend more money on them.

IN TRAY

1 What fixed costs does Aaron have?

2 What will happen to the amount Aaron spends on raw materials as he produces more items of furniture?

3 How do you think Aaron is able to compete with larger furniture manufacturers?

ACTION

Which of the inputs of your local supermarket are likely to be variable costs?

The cost of the wood, the glue and all the other things Aaron uses to make his furniture will go up each time he makes another item. These are known as **variable costs** because they vary with the number of items produced. If there is no output, variable costs will be zero.

The followings costs are variable costs for most businesses.

◆ **Raw materials**
These are the materials used in the production process. As more items are produced, more raw materials are used and more money is spent on buying them.

◆ **Energy (electricity and gas)**
In a manufacturing business the machines that produce the goods need power. If the machines are used more in order to produce more items, this cost will rise.

◆ **Wages**

In some businesses employees are paid a wage that may change week by week or month by month. They may be paid overtime for doing extra work, or piece rates, where they are paid for the number of items they produce.

Wages can be fixed or variable costs. Tracey and her helper (see page 222) treated their pay as a fixed cost because without them, there would be no business at all! The pay of people who are hired to do a particular job may sometimes be treated as a variable cost.

Aaron's variable costs

On average, Aaron spends £85 for each new piece of furniture on raw materials and power. This does not include his own wages. He relies on the profit to provide him with an income.

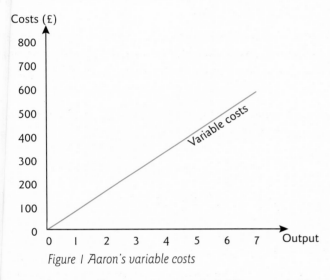

Figure 1 Aaron's variable costs

Aaron's total costs

Total costs can be calculated by adding fixed and variable costs together. Figure 2 shows how total costs can be represented. Aaron's fixed costs are £90 per week, which is mainly rent.

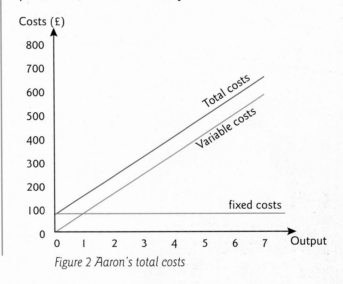

Figure 2 Aaron's total costs

Figure 1 shows an example of how variable costs can be represented. As output increases, the costs increase.

IN TRAY

1 What would happen to Aaron's costs if his rent rose by £30 per week?

2 How would costs change if Aaron took on an assistant at busy times?

3 Tracey had fixed costs of £575 per week. Her variable costs were quite low – just £1 per haircut. Draw a graph showing her fixed, variable and total costs. Assume the most she can do in one week is 150 haircuts. Do you think she is going to be able to make a profit?

KEY TERMS

🔑 **Variable costs** are costs that rise as the level of output rises.

🔑 **Total costs** are the fixed costs plus the variable costs.

34 Will we break even?

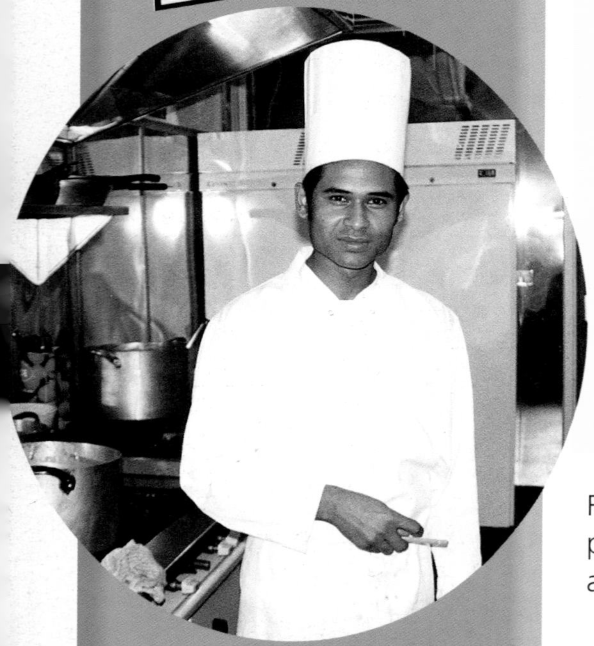

How many do we need to sell?

The Rickshaw is a very popular Asian takeaway. A family-run business, it sells a range of Tandoori, Balti and Bangladeshi curries as well as starters and side dishes. Some evenings business is slow, but it becomes very busy on Fridays and Saturdays. The family has bought the premises, and has a mortgage.

The owner finds it useful to know how many meals have to be made in order to make a profit. This will obviously depend on the costs of the business, both fixed and variable. It will also depend on a third factor – revenue. Revenue is the amount of money coming into the business and will depend on the selling price of the meals. The price of meals varies from around £3.65 for a vegetarian Balti to £6.95 for a Tandoori King Prawn Masala.

The sons of the family work in the shop for a wage, which is treated as a variable cost since it depends on how much work there is. The owner relies on the profit for his income.

IN TRAY

1   Make a list of the Rickshaw's fixed and variable costs.

2   Why does the owner want to know how many meals he needs to sell in order to make a profit?

For the takeaway, revenue depends on the selling price of each item produced and the number of meals sold. If the selling price per meal is, on average, £4, the **total revenue** will be as shown in the table.

This is shown in the graph in Figure 1.

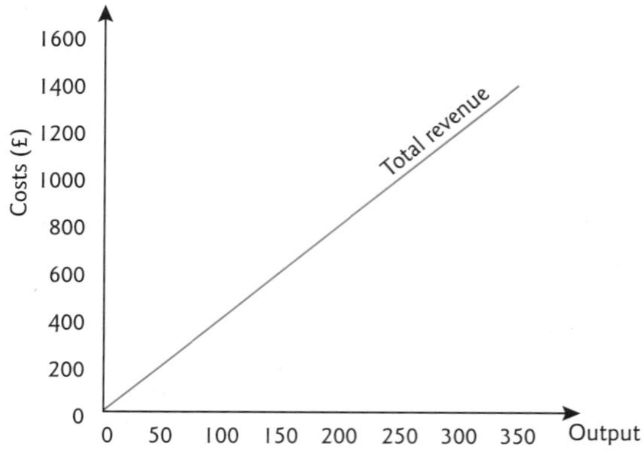

PORTFOLIO PROMPTS

Find out from a business you are studying whether the idea of breakeven is useful to the management. Explain how the business might calculate it. If the cost and revenue figures are available, put them on a spreadsheet and use it to do the calculations.

Figure 1 Total revenue

Total revenue	
Output	Revenue
0	0
50	200
100	400
150	600
200	800
250	1,000
300	1,200
350	1,400

The idea of breakeven helps businesses to work out what their output needs to be to make a profit. The **breakeven point** is the point at which the business is taking enough money to cover all of its costs. At that output it is making neither a profit nor a loss.

A simple way to calculate the breakeven point is as follows.

$$\text{The breakeven point} = \frac{\text{fixed costs}}{(\text{selling price per unit} - \text{variable costs per unit})}$$

Let's work out an example for the Rickshaw.

◆ The average price charged for a meal is £4, so the selling price = £4.

◆ The fixed costs are £120 per week.

◆ The variable costs are £3 per meal.

$$\text{The breakeven point} = \frac{120}{4-3}$$

$$= \frac{120}{1}$$

$$= 120 \text{ meals}$$

Figure 2 Breakeven chart

A C T I O N

The Rickshaw will soon have paid off its mortgage, which will mean that fixed costs fall to £60 per week. Reproduce the cost and revenue table using the new figures. Calculate the breakeven point and draw a graph to represent it.

Therefore the breakeven point is 120 meals. This means that if the takeaway sells 120 meals it will break even – it will have enough sales revenue to cover its costs. If it sells fewer, it will make a loss. If it sells more, it will make a profit.

Breakeven chart				
Output	Fixed costs	Variable costs	Total costs	Revenue
0	120	0	120	0
50	120	150	270	200
100	120	300	420	400
150	120	450	570	600
200	120	600	720	800
250	120	750	870	1,000
300	120	900	1,020	1,200
350	120	1,050	1,170	1,400

We can use these figures to plot a graph.

The graph will look like this:

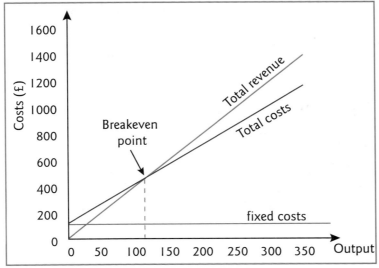

Figure 3 Breakeven point

K E Y   T E R M S

⚷ **Total revenue** is the amount of money coming into a business – the number of items sold multiplied by the selling price.

⚷ The **breakeven point** is the output at which the total revenue is exactly equal to the total costs.

35 All change

OBJECTIVES

To find out what happens to the breakeven point when there are changes in costs and revenues.

What happens?

As we have already seen, it is useful for the owner of the Rickshaw to know what the breakeven level of output is. However, a problem that any business faces is that things never stay the same for long. Ingredients for the curries are bought from a wholesaler and sometimes the owner finds that prices have gone up. Of course, there are times when the costs of ingredients might go down. Nevertheless, any change in these costs will have an effect on the breakeven point.

Sales revenue may change, too. If the local fish and chip shop closes down, more customers may come in.

IN TRAY

1 What might cause a change in the Rickshaw's fixed costs?
2 What might cause a change in the Rickshaw's variable costs?
3 Can you think of any other changes that might take place which would affect the breakeven point?

ACTION

Calculate the breakeven point and draw a graph showing costs, revenue and the breakeven level of output when:

◆ fixed costs = £120

◆ variable costs = £3 per item

◆ selling price = £5 per item

Now calculate the breakeven point and draw graphs to show each of the following changes to the original situation:

(a) fixed costs rise to £150

(b) variable costs rise to £4 per meal

(c) selling price rises to £6 per meal

Would you suggest a change in price to the management of the Rickshaw? Explain your reasoning.

There are three possible changes that can affect the breakeven level of output. The first two involve a change in costs – fixed or variable – and the business has little control over these changes. The third involves a change in selling price. This is something which the business can decide for itself.

Let's see what happens when changes take place.

In the beginning

The Rickshaw starts out with the following costs and price:

Fixed costs = £120

Variable costs = £3 per item

Selling price = £4 per item

Breakeven = 120/4 − 3 = 120 items

The business has to sell 120 items to break even.

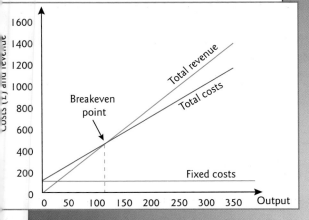

Scenario 1

The cost of the mortgage has risen. Fixed costs are now £150.

Fixed costs = £150

Variable costs = £3 per item

Selling price = £4 per item

Breakeven = 150/4 − 3 = 150 items

The business now has to sell 150 meals to break even.

Notice that a rise in fixed costs:

♦ makes the fixed cost line move up

♦ makes the total cost line move up

♦ makes the breakeven level of output higher.

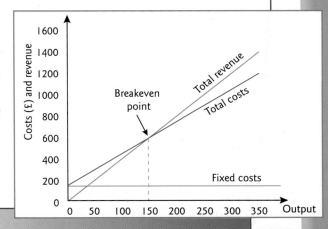

Scenario 2

The cost of ingredients goes up: variable costs rise to £3.50 per meal.

Fixed costs = £120

Variable costs = £3.50 per item

Selling price = £4 per item

Breakeven = 120/4 − 3.50 = 240 items

The business would have to sell 240 meals to break even.

Notice that a rise in variable costs:

♦ makes the variable cost line steeper

♦ makes the breakeven point higher.

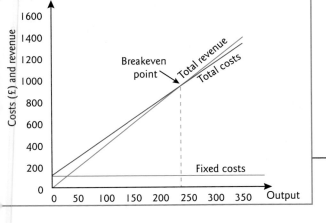

Scenario 3

The Rickshaw decides to put up prices: the average selling price rises to £4.50.

Fixed costs = £120

Variable costs = £3

Selling price = £4.50

Breakeven = 120/4.50 − 3 = 80 items

Now the business only has to sell 80 meals to break even.

Notice that a rise in the selling price:

♦ makes the revenue line steeper

♦ makes the breakeven point lower.

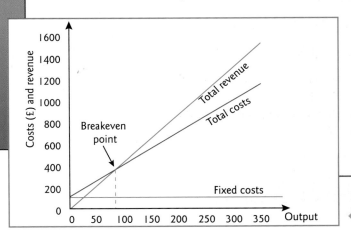